INFLUENCE

ACROSS

BOUNDARIES

INFLUENCE
ACROSS
BOUNDARIES

How to Succeed in a
Global Business Environment

Helen Baxter-Southworth

Third Bridge Press
Arnold, Maryland

Third Bridge Press
1290 Bay Dale Drive, #323
Arnold, MD 21012
www.thirdbridgepress.com

Ordering Information
Quantity sales. Special discounts are available on quantity purchases by corporations, associations, and others. For details, contact the "Special Sales Department" at the Third Bridge Press address above.

Individual sales. Third Bridge Press publications are available through most bookstores. They can also be ordered directly from Third Bridge Press at the address above.

Orders by US trade bookstores and wholesalers. Please contact Cardinal Publishers Group: Tel: (800) 296-0481; Fax: (317) 879-0872; www.cardinalpub .com.

Printed in the United States of America

Cataloging in Publication
Baxter-Southworth, Helen.
    Influence across boundaries : how to succeed in a global business environment / Helen Baxter-Southworth.
    p. cm.
    Includes bibliographical references and index.
    ISBN 978-0-9820569-2-9
1. International business enterprises. 2. Success in business. 3. Intercultural communication. 4. International trade. 5. International finance. 6. Investments, Foreign. 7. International economic relations. 8. Globalization—Economic aspects. I. Title.
HF1379.B39   2011
658/.049—dc22   2011928358

FIRST EDITION

Cover design: Kuo Design
Interior design and composition: Bev Butterfield, Girl of the West Productions
Editing: PeopleSpeak

This book is dedicated to my husband, Chas,
as a sign of my love and appreciation.
His encouragement and sense of humor
throughout the learning, teaching, and
writing part of my life are true gifts.

Contents

Acknowledgments

I am grateful to the managers who have participated in the past eight years of small coaching groups designed as part of culture change efforts. Your stories, struggles, and successes informed and validated the five resources of influence across boundaries contained in this book. These small group forums were originally part of a concerted effort to transform IT into a more business-oriented function. You were asked to sell rather than explain, to speak "commercial" rather than IT. For many of you, this was easy enough—you already spoke two and three and four languages. But to let go of informing for persuading? This was a huge leap of faith. To go from long-winded process diagrams to getting concisely to the heart of the matter with the listener's interests in mind? This was painful, rewarding, and sometimes even fun. Thank you for sharing your dilemmas, risking potential humiliation and loss of face with peers who were learning to influence along with you. Your trust and willingness to challenge yourselves continues to inspire me.

When the ante was upped by a more urgent mission—to eliminate regional autonomy and save billions in expense dollars by standardizing technology on a global enterprise level—everything changed. Influential communication was required, yes, but across geographic boundaries while a new matrix structure was being built and before standardization budgets were in place. We learned together that designing the right architecture and operating model by the book and with the counsel of the best information systems research scientists is one thing. Leading this change globally is quite another. I knew you had the texts and counsel of leading information systems research scientists in one hand. I wanted you to have another book that honored the leadership required in your other hand.

Thank you, Roberta Shwartz, for generously sharing your business wisdom—learned at your father's side. Thank you, Rick, for your insight and to Ken and Andrew for your commitment to cultural change.

As *Influence Across Boundaries* began to take form, several international leaders and enthusiasts shared their stories along the way. Thank you to all of you who told the stories that found their way in some form into the case studies that illustrate the art of influencing across boundaries. Thank you, Trish Myers, Deborra Clark Oser, and Terry Kaufmann, for joining me in the initial launch of *Influence Across Boundaries* in London. I would not have stepped out on this edge if you had not been there with me.

I want to acknowledge the sixty women in the original Women's Leadership Collaboration five-year program. We taught each other about self-authorization, telling the truth as we know it, and the realities of dominate-subordinate dynamics. You encouraged my dream of writing. Thank you for the steadfast faith and leadership of Joyce Weir and Alexandra Merrill and to the women of Vanderbent—Judith Leibowitz, Bobbie O'Conner, Teressa Moore Griffin, Rita Andrews, and Anne Litwin—for your integrity and humor regarding all things women and personal growth. Thank you to Judith Leibowitz for leading me into women's work. Thank you, Teressa Moore Griffin, for encouraging me to write and get the book published. And you, Rebecca Ripley, for reading the card that says "Be swift."

I also want to thank my dear friend Marilyn Petersen for her immense generosity of spirit for inviting me along on her vacations and allowing me the time and space to set up desks with the best views on earth to write.

Thank you to the executive teams that were committed and trusting clients. You gave me the chance to work with Russ Forrester—my first psychometrician—to devise an intervention and instrument to help you "put your money where your mouth is" around the importance of collaboration. The results of this research are contained within this book.

The final push to write this book came from several sources I wish to acknowledge: Walter Holloway's statement "Just start writing; I know you've got the book inside your head" and Tina Corner's introduction to Marty O'Neill and his gracious invitation to publish with him at Third Bridge Press.

I am indebted to you, Sharon Goldinger, for expert, thorough, and patient editorial support and guidance. Your unambiguous suggestions for improvement and clear expectations and standards helped turn what I thought might be a book into the book before us.

Finally, I want to thank my family, Chas, and Jesse and Emily, for your love and presence as I wrote. You carried on as a miraculously harmonious family around me and without me but within earshot, which provided the loving support I required. Chas, your strength and humor carried me.

Delivering Results in a Complex International Organization

Every multinational organization is complex. As an individual and as a leader in such an organization, you struggle with those complexities every day. And your difficulties are increased whenever you think you are the only international manager facing these challenges.

What is the cause of this complexity? As you are well aware, in order to reduce costs, companies have reorganized themselves to share very expensive resources. You may or may not have heard your organization referred to as a "matrix" organization. It was originally restructured to share the services of the "vertical" functions (for example, IT, finance, marketing, and HR) with all the "horizontal" lines of business. A particular line of business can no longer remain virtually autonomous, decentralized, or "siloed" with its own HR department, its own finance department, its own legal department, and so on. Everyone everywhere shares all services. This vertical-horizontal crossing of lines creates the image of a two-dimensional grid or matrix, which gives the structure its name.

A matrix organization is structured not only to share expensive and highly specialized staff and equipment but also to be able to quickly redistribute them to a line of business that encounters an expected or unexpected opportunity or threat. For example, having one set of highly trained finance specialists who can be deployed on an as-needed basis is less costly than duplicating these same capabilities within each business line. No single line of business "owns"

1

these expert resources; the costs can be shared. The finance person on loan to one line of business still reports to her finance manager, but she also has a temporary, "dotted-line" manager in the business who will pay for the services on an as-needed basis. The matrix structure is distinguished by these dual reporting relationships, and this is where the matrix begins to get its reputation for complexity. Having two managers can create role ambiguity and reporting confusion, and both managers must be consulted when a decision is made about the finance person's performance rating.

The addition of geographic markets adds a third dimension. Now specialists and resources can be flexibly distributed as needed to all lines of business in every regional market or they can focus locally and tailor their services to their particular customers' needs. This is often referred to as a "global-local model."

Add customer segmentation to your strategy, and lines of business can share customer information, referrals, income, and relationship management across business product lines that share the same type of customer. Customers may be segmented by wealth, age, or affinities, for example. Your structure now has a fourth dimension.

Although cultures and languages are not part of a formal organization chart or operating model, diversity adds another layer of complexity. Add to this global, regional, and national stability, economic and market trends, regulatory and trade guidelines, tax policies, health policies, human relations, and social practices, and the multidimensional international organization is born.

A profitable international organization must be designed so that the organization's rich resources can be flexibly shifted from one product line to another based on emerging needs in the marketplace. Flexibility speeds response to competitive conditions, technology trends, and breakthroughs.

Like any other complex system, an international organization requires some unique policies, procedures, and leadership practices. In order to get work done within a matrix organization, you will exert more influence than you will authority. Lines of authority are shared at best, blurred at worst. Resources are shifted based on opportunity and rarely owned outright. Cooperation is prized and never taken for granted because it can't be mandated. Power is constantly being rebalanced. Collaboration is as much about knowing how to engage in constructive conflict as it is about focusing on collective results and building trust.

Dynamics of a Complex International Organization

To get results in this environment, you first need to understand the dynamics of a complex international organization. Then you need a shared vocabulary, a way to talk about the complexities with others. Finally, you need to master the five resources for influence, which is key to getting results in a matrix organization. Let's begin with a closer look at the dynamics of a complex multinational organization, which include multiple managers, power imbalances, and structural complexity.

Multiple Managers

The dual or multiple chains of command is the distinguishing characteristic of the matrix structure. One person may report to a regional manager on a local project, to a business manager for a business project, and to a global manager on a global project. Others may report to the manager of the functional department they represent and to another manager in the product or business unit. Cross-functional team assignments, temporary job transfers, a series of rotating managers, overseas assignments—all of these are possible changes to your reporting relationships in a global business.

Power Imbalances

Sharing resources across functions and businesses provides optimum flexibility to adjust to changes in the marketplace. This means the power inherent in temporarily "owning" these rich resources will shift regularly. The decision-making power over resources can shift for a number of reasons. For example, if a temporary or devastating crisis occurs—regional, market, social, or environmental—or if competition grows or the market shifts, interest in or demand for certain products and services may be temporarily de-emphasized. Another product or service must be mobilized to temporarily take up the slack and bring in the revenue that supports the other lines of business. Resource authority also shifts as one region's economy contracts and another emerges or as one region is invested in and another region's budget allocation is put on hold.

The power of technology is evident in its enormous budget, the number of business personnel dedicated to technology-related teams, and the time allocated to its discussion in every executive meeting. Each time technology is identified as a business solution, its power grows. In the same way, as regulatory oversight increases, the compliance function gains more power to audit, delay, or terminate a procedure or a customer segment that is deemed risky.

Power imbalances are frequent in the matrix organization, and top managers are responsible for creating some reasonable semblance of a balance of power. For example, they can recalibrate power using pay, job titles, access to most senior managers, or reporting level within a hierarchy.[1]

Structural Complexity

In a matrix organization, work is spread among multiple initiatives, programs, and project teams with overlapping interests of a variety of sponsors, sources of funds, and stakeholders. Imagine an organization spread across India, Hong Kong, and North America with two different product lines of business. As functional specialists are temporarily shared across regions and lines of business, it becomes extremely challenging to allocate the time and expenses of all these employees.

Structural complexity increases because the input of so many people—from various functions, lines of business, and regions—must be taken into account. They are all weighing in on decisions that impact their areas of interest using different procedures, processes, and terminology for recording and reporting information, which adds to the potential for confusion.

The matrix organization's structure gives employees a greater sense of complexity than any other organizational design. Rightly or wrongly, people can feel powerless to change the system. They might complain of "procedural delays," "red tape," and the general frustrations of being in a large organization.[2]

In addition, geographically dispersed "virtual" teams across time zones allow employees to maintain 24/7 global market coverage. This "always open" model inevitably jeopardizes people's sense of work-life balance. On the other hand, many workers enjoy the challenges and the variety of opportunities of working internationally in such a complex organization. "I am never bored," they report.

The Value of a Shared Vocabulary

Understanding the complexities of a matrix organization is just the first step. You need to acknowledge and be able to talk about these challenges with your team. Developing a shared vocabulary can be enormously helpful.

Recently I worked in a two-day off-site with a team of executives in an international organization and their teams of managers. I was asked to initiate a series of conversations to assist them in clarifying their strategy.

I promised to give them a brief description of the organization in which they might be working and then let them discuss the implications among themselves. I started by explaining that I had given a similar description to another group of international managers the week before and a manager was astounded by how much I knew about his company.

"I don't know a lot about your company in particular," I said. "I just know something about the dynamics of an international organization and how it might feel to deliver results."

Using a blank whiteboard, I started with the introduction to the international business organization and its environment that you have just read.

After fifteen minutes, I asked the managers to talk among themselves about whether this description was accurate and, if so, how having this perspective and contextual background might help them do their jobs. They were so appreciative to have their world described and work contextualized—and to realize there was some "science" behind a structure that felt less-than-perfect or "artless." Once their complex reporting relationships were explained, they no longer felt like their organization had a dysfunctional communication style or a penchant for meetings run amuck.

This brief discussion gave them a shared vocabulary to use for the rest of the meeting—just as this book will give you a shared vocabulary you can use with your team. And more than that, they developed an appreciation for the difficulty of creating a "perfect" structure. They felt far more ownership of the dimensions and dilemmas of their structure. I heard a lot more about what "we" need to do and a lot less about what "they" are doing to us.

From there, I outlined the five resources in this book. These are resources that many of them have already been using to successfully deliver results. But everyone who expects to deliver results without the formal authority to command and control the behaviors and attitudes of others will recognize the complex, multidimensional structure of a multinational organization and the need to use influence across multiple boundaries.

Leadership and Influence

The ability to influence across multiple boundaries—to align a diverse global team distributed across all time zones—requires a unique set of knowledge, skills, and abilities. To communicate a compelling and unifying vision across native languages, to generate a shared sense of urgency across cultures, and to build commitment to a common set of priorities across regions and lines of business is a challenge for even the most agile and adept international manager.

In a traditional organization, managers are formally given status and authority to hire, fire, rate performance, make assignments, set pay, and promote. In the dual- and multiple-manager structure used in complex international organizations, however, reporting lines are blurred because employees formally report to two or more managers.

In this book, the term "manager" refers to those individuals who are formally authorized and written into an organization chart. Managers at the top will be referred to as "executives" and "senior managers" or by their formal designations—president, CEO, CTSO, and so on. The term "leader" will refer to those individuals with or without formal rank who authorize themselves to influence others and have come to be identified as leaders by many others. Unlike traditional managers, leaders at all levels operate without formal positions of authority.

Without formal authority to command and control the actions of others, leaders must use influence, sway, and persuasion to change people's minds, hearts, attitudes, and behavior to achieve results. To get things done, leaders depend on their informal networks and personal resources.

Influence is the skill of leaders. Influencing the attitudes and behaviors of others—without formal authority—requires the ability to build rapport, establish credibility, assess and align mutual interests, and manage agreement and conflict. In a multinational environment, influence requires sensitivity to cultural differences.

To be effective across cultures, you will need cultural intelligence, a broad understanding of the values and practices of the various dimensions of culture, and the ability to communicate so that you include, understand, and are understood across cultures. However, like most leaders, you probably do not have the time or the opportunity to learn cross-cultural influence skills through years of firsthand global travel experience, conducting business across international boundaries, or immersion courses. Giving you the resources you need in a short time frame is the purpose of this book.

About "Boundaries"

Some managers object to the term "boundaries." As one very outspoken and very senior executive told me, "We don't have *boundaries* in this organization." He considered the term an inaccurate and negative characterization of his company. In the context of this book, boundaries are any performance inhibitor, any hurdle, challenge, or question you will have to address and resolve to close a performance gap. Boundaries can be internal to individuals—their personal resources, knowledge, skills, or abilities. On the other hand, boundaries may be external to the individual and related to the organization's environment and resources. Examples of external, systemic boundaries include

- The way a company is formally structured
- Its procedures for measuring and rewarding performance
- Its policies about interacting with customers
- The quality and availability of its tools and equipment
- The compatibility of technologies available to share information and get work done across regions
- The regional markets in which the company competes
- Geographic time zones that cause conflict with traditional work hours
- Unique environmental, economic, and labor regulations of the organization or the host nation
- Cultural norms and assumptions about authority, teamwork, giving direct feedback, or how to communicate

Here is an example of the kinds of boundaries that sometimes need to be crossed. Over eight years ago, a regional chief information officer in a large multinational organization and his director of organization and leadership development came to me and a business partner with an exciting proposition. Were we interested in working with them in transforming their IT culture? The CIO witnessed daily a breakdown in the communication between their technology managers and their commercial business counterparts. Technology was on every executive's weekly agenda and taking a disproportionate amount of their valuable time together, but little understanding or agreement resulted. This communication breakdown was costing everyone in time, mistakes, and resources. Worse than this, a breakdown in trust, along with frustration, tension, and a clear "we-they" mentality, was developing. Special "business-technology liaisons" had to be created to serve as translators between the technology managers and their business counterparts.

Cross-culturally, the technology and business leaders had very different perspectives of time and urgency. The technology professionals thought in terms of the multiple quarters or years required to create the solutions the business partners required. Each time they bent to the business side's pressure and cobbled some application together, they were convinced they were causing another problem down the road that their peers somewhere in the world would eventually have to correct.

The business leaders, on the other hand, measured performance in the shortest increments of time—weeks, months, and quarters. They needed solutions—now. They witnessed the problems of technology every time a customer transaction failed or a system was down. Their time and attention were on the results, the bottom line, and the impact of these technologies, not their architecture.

From a communication perspective, the challenge was the language, thinking process, and influence style of each group. The technology professionals thought in terms of cause and effect. They followed step-by-step processes to achieve the outcome their end-users demanded. Their business partners, on the other hand, spoke about customers and wallet share, not users. They thought in terms of costs, benefits, and outcomes, not processes. And they had to acquire and retain customers who had a choice, not please a captive, in-house audience.

In addition, cultural dimensions were added to the business-functional differences as goals and customers were shared across businesses and continents. Specialists from India, China, Vietnam,

Brazil, Malaysia, Indonesia, Mexico, and North America needed to achieve results together. Finally, the groups faced fundamental misunderstandings about where initiatives were positioned within the strategy of the formal and informal organization and their strategic and political priority.

For over twenty-two years I have coached people in international organizations like this. Their pragmatic approach to overcome challenges has taught me the "art" of delivering results across multiple boundaries. I witnessed how formal authority was no longer a card to be played, how people could successfully influence across boundaries, and how much personal stretch and fortitude were required. The "science" I can share assures them their experiences are more than random occurrences and can reduce the stress that comes from thinking they are alone. In turn, they are able to coach their coworkers using a common language, to give a name to what they were experiencing, and to offer information about the practices and lessons of others. This is the niche I serve and what I have a great passion to discuss with you.

The Resources You Need

The huge amount of information coming into a large and complex international organization from its external and internal environments adds to an already high-pressure climate. While information is crucial if a global organization is to remain competitive, information overload makes it impossible for executive teams to make all key decisions in a timely manner. Decisions must be distributed. Conflicts and debate must be encouraged. This inherently challenging and high-pressure environment may be further exacerbated when conflicts do not come to light or when resources—and the power to control them—must be redistributed. Creating an organizational culture of collaboration and cooperation and providing an open forum for debate and healthy conflict is a tall order.

To successfully influence results, an international manager requires a unique set of resources. Influence without authority in a complex international organization requires more than your personal ability to persuade others. It requires the ability to strategically position your initiative, successfully interact with people of diverse cultures, collaborate and manage conflict, and leverage your personal network of connections.

The purpose of this book is to support people who are managing initiatives of critical importance to an international organization but whose authority is not clearly identified within the hierarchy of the organization. Formally recognized position and status in an organization are very important to doing business in many cultures. However, in an international organization's complex shared services or matrix structure, formal status and authority are shared and obscured. We will discuss the resources you will want to develop to be an influential and collaborative leader when you don't have the formal, command-and-control authority that position and budget often convey.

This book is written for you

- If you must deliver results across multiple boundaries: geographic, regional, lines of business, function, culture, language

- If you must influence a high degree of cooperation without direct control, formal authority, or position power

- If your span of control or influence does not necessarily include formally dedicated resources, budget, or the authority to rate the performance of those you depend on to get the job done

This book discusses the resources you will need to develop to influence across boundaries and deliver results and the activities, tools, and best practices you can apply today. And just as important, it also identifies external factors in the organizational environment that can restrain your performance and that you must take into account.

You will find pragmatic tools you can use to deliver results and mobilize commitment across multiple boundaries. You will identify best practices to strategically position your initiative, build cooperative relationships, influence across cultures, and build a network of effective connections within a matrix organization. You will be guided to clarify your personal strengths and develop a plan to influence change across the organization. Finally, you will find ways to develop a personal network and strategy to effectively influence, communicate with, and align diverse business partners.

The core of the book presents the science and art of five critical "resources for results":

- *Strategic positioning:* How to influence an outcome by favorably positioning and communicating your idea, project, or initiative within an organization

- *Cross-cultural know-how:* How to communicate in a way that includes and can be understood by people of other cultures, languages, and diversity factors in a manner that recognizes, affirms, and values the worth of the individual

- *Personal influence and persuasion:* How to effectively apply a variety of strategies to appeal to the hearts and minds of a diverse audience to influence their attitudes and behaviors toward the goal

- *Collaboration and conflict management:* How to win the cooperation of others using alternative bargaining and conflict management styles and how to maintain relationships while managing agreement and differences

- *Personal network and connections:* How to create and effectively use a personal, professional network of connections to identify opportunities, get the best information and the most cost-effective resources, and establish credibility outside traditional organizational or market structures

For the convenience of explanation and development, each of these five resources is discussed individually. But in application, these resources complement and overlap each other.

Within each chapter a scan of related research and theory is provided as the science for each resource. The art is represented by a set of suggested actions, tools, and best practices.

Each resource will be introduced with its own brief "Big Picture Scan" with questions to ask yourself about that resource. You may recognize yourself or a member of your team in these questions.

Each resource is illustrated by a case study of a real-life individual or team that succeeded in delivering results by influencing across boundaries. The case studies will give you a chance to learn from peers in similar circumstances with similar issues. You will also discover that you are not the only one experiencing these challenges. Unless specifically indicated, all the names of people and organizations in the case studies are fictional and their stories are composites of individuals and companies.

Each of these five resources has been the subject of extensive multidisciplinary research over many years and across the globe in fields such as social psychology, organization development, behavior science, international business, and cultural intelligence. The book offers a high-level review of this research and provides a common and accepted language in which to describe the resource and presents practical and field-tested actions.

The theories of the science will engage your rational thinking, and the practices and case studies will illustrate the theory in practice. You will see situations and problems you are familiar with but have never put a name to. This will increase your effectiveness as a coach to others on your team.

This book is like a personal consultation on your own challenge. It is designed to stimulate insights to help you achieve your objectives. It will help you identify areas you will want to revisit in your project plans. You will better understand how you are communicating with native and nonnative English speakers and learn practical tips to apply immediately to improve your comprehensibility. You will have personal takeaways and a clear sense of next steps so you can confidently plot your next influence strategy.

The appendices offer you resources you can refer to as your needs change with each new assignment. In appendix A, you'll discover how to scan the setting in which you will be working so you can anticipate boundaries you will need to cross. Appendix B provides a simple formula for a persuasive business case to win others over. Appendix C offers a last-minute checklist for influence planning—important questions to ask yourself before walking out the door. Appendix D is an additional audience assessment you can use to confirm you know your audience sufficiently to influence them. Finally, a reading reference and resource list will help you learn more about the science behind the art of each resource.

As you and your team develop these five personal resources, I hope you will feel more confident in your ability to be an influential innovator and entrepreneur and be better able to deliver results internationally. Let's begin with a look at the first influence resource: strategic positioning.

One

Improving Your Strategic Positioning

Strategic positioning is the ability to influence an outcome by favorably positioning and communicating an idea, project, or initiative within an organization. In this chapter we will explore the importance of strategic positioning in a complex and ever-changing international organization. We will also look at the costs of failing to position an idea or initiative. You will find practical and proven methods, tools, and best practices to influence the outcome by favorably positioning your initiative.

Big Picture Scan

Before you read on, answer these questions:

- Have you ever become so busy you have neglected communicating with one of your managers or key stakeholders?
- Have you ever accomplished something of value that no one even knew about?
- Have you ever had your idea taken over by someone else?
- Have you ever resisted advertising your success because you worried about being perceived as a self-promoter or not a team player?
- Have you ever been left out of an important meeting?
- Have you ever lost momentum in a project just when you thought you were making great progress?

All of these problems are the result of a failure in strategic positioning. One chief executive likens strategic positioning in a global organization to a game on a large chessboard or checkerboard that represents the setting or situation of her business initiative. She envisions the entire game board first, considers her long-term goal, and maps out her strategy before she makes her first move. Sometimes she plays a deliberate and complex game of chess; other times she plays a quick game of checkers. But she always expects the game board to change constantly with her opponent's moves. She stays well informed of what's going on—on the entire board, not just with her project.

Four Key Elements of Strategic Positioning

Strategic positioning is a vital skill in influencing across boundaries. Effective strategic positioning requires four key elements: organizational know-how, political savvy, stakeholder communication, and the ability to sustain change.

- *Organizational know-how:* Organizational know-how is your knowledge about how organizations work in general and about your own organization's interests, strategy, structure, and policies. It is critical to effectively delivering results within the *formal* organization. Your organizational know-how will provide you with the essential understanding of where your initiative fits within the big picture of your organization. It will also provide you with a clear line of sight to the local and global objectives your initiative supports. Knowing the policies, procedures, and other supporting mechanisms of your organization will help you use them to your advantage or work to change them when they are an impediment.

- *Political savvy:* Political savvy is the ability to understand how to get things done in your organization in an *informal* sense. It includes knowing who the opinion leaders are, which decision makers to turn to for advice, and how to build coalitions to exert power and influence as a group rather than trying to go it alone. Political savvy is your ability to get things done in the complex organizational maze—both inside and outside formal channels—effectively and quietly for maximum benefit.

- *Stakeholder communication:* Many groups and individuals may stand to gain or lose from the changes your initiative includes. Stakeholders are those who have an interest in, who benefit or lose from, or who depend on the success of your initiative. Stakeholder communication is your motivation and ability to influence those who have an interest in your initiative and who may bring pressure to bear on your resources and critical decisions. Your ability to communicate with key stakeholders and manage your relationships with them is crucial to the long-term viability of your innovation or initiative.

- *The ability to sustain change:* To sustain change means to deliver results in the present that are able to persist in the future. It requires that you be able to formally and officially build into your initiative future funding, maintenance costs, and required human and material resources; create systems, policies, and procedures that formalize or institutionalize your initiative; account for your initiative's impact on other parts of the organization; and minimize resistance so that your initiative will endure into the future.

CASE STUDY
Scott Farris and Strategic Positioning

You can enhance your perspective and the strategic position of your project or initiative within your larger organization in many ways. To illustrate each of the four components of strategic positioning, let's follow one international manager as he seeks to better position his programs and projects within his organization. For each strategic positioning challenge he faces, we will outline some specific coaching advice.

Scott Farris is a senior business manager in a large international bank. Like many large organizations, his bank is in the midst of a massive restructuring, moving from a collection of locally oriented banking businesses to one bank with one shared business strategy and a common technology and operational infrastructure.

The restructuring means Scott will need to work on updating his organizational know-how. He will want to learn the origin and the rationale of the restructuring strategy; investigate existing and new, related policies; and understand if and where his projects and initiatives fit in the big picture. Scott could select a mentor with better and broader knowledge of the organization. Better yet, he could select several "composite" mentors to ensure the broadest perspective of the organization outside his immediate area of concern.

This vision of a globally unified bank has set high and urgent expectations. To effectively compete and win in today's economy *while restructuring* involves so many moving parts, it is, as one executive told me, "like the ancient Chinese art of spinning plates." The standardization of decentralized, independent, regionally embedded processes, procedures, and systems requires intense cooperation. More people will be involved in decision making. Tensions will be high, internal competition for valuable resources fierce, and accountability ambiguous.

Scott's political savvy is in play here. Scott will do well to understand the current pressures and interests of each of his diverse stakeholders. After making a thorough list of all his key stakeholders, he should arrange to speak with them to uncover their vested interests in his initiative and find out about other initiatives in which they are involved. He should take advantage of these conversations to select whom to ask which questions about how to use the informal system to get the job done. For example, he could ask one stakeholder about her favorite way to promote her initiative without appearing too self-interested. He could ask another which are the most popular initiatives. With another, he might ask how she aligns her initiatives with the more popular initiatives.

Scott's organizational know-how is also in play because a complex shared services or matrix organization is designed to shift resources from one unit to another. This shift of resources and priorities means the "power of the purse" will shift and knock power off-balance.

Because of the multiple reporting lines inherent in the matrix structure of his bank, Scott has a variety of direct, solid-line managers and indirect or dotted-line managers. These interested parties may at any time bring pressure to bear on his resources and decisions concerning his initiatives.

Again, Scott's organizational know-how is in play. Scott will need to refresh his understanding of the predictable dynamics of the shared services or matrix organization. This structure is complex and confusing. The multiple reporting lines of this organizational design create role and accountability confusion and require greater coordination between all those who will participate in making decisions—which slows decision times. These dynamics will be magnified during this period of transformation.

Scott has always been aware that not all stakeholders are created equal. Each believes he or she is entitled to different and special considerations. Scott admits he enjoys the valuable professional exposure he gets while working for a wide variety of top executives and the excitement of bigger strategic perspectives at the top. However, Scott also feels the anxiety of risking any one stakeholder's dissatisfaction as different demands so often compete for the time of his already-stretched team.

Scott will want to learn which initiatives or priorities are most likely to conflict or compete with his for limited resources.

Scott felt the sting of miscalculating this balancing act in his last performance rating. He spent the lion's share of his personal time and communication with a new executive leading a popular new program. This new program was not formally listed in Scott's performance agreements, however, and the executive he did please had no say in his performance rating. Seduced by the excitement and strategic importance of this popular new initiative, Scott made a strategic error in neglecting his formal manager and her manager. And though he made a new contact and supporter on the one hand, his formal managers felt neglected, were unaware of his achievements, and downgraded his overall performance.

Scott's stakeholder communication has diminished, and he needs to execute a "stakeholder recovery plan." From his complete list of his key stakeholders, he must identify those who could be better informed. He should reinstate regular biweekly or monthly calls so that he can listen to and inform his managers and stakeholders. Scott will need to capture the attention of these busy and potentially soured stakeholders and concisely deliver a memorable message that appeals directly to their self-interests. He should also enlarge his base of support. Rather than repeatedly going back to the same senior executives for their acknowledgment and support, he can make another list that identifies the opinion leaders at the lowest possible level in the organization and the trusted advisors the senior executives turn to when making decisions.

Unfortunately for Scott, the organization's new strategy was not in his performance agreement (his "balanced scorecard")—or anyone else's in that first year of its launch. As a result, everyone that jumped enthusiastically into this strategy was penalized. From a sustainability perspective, Scott will want to formally include this new initiative in his and his team's balanced scorecards. He will avoid future confusion by clarifying the relative weight or percentage of his ratings tied to this initiative and who will rate his performance on this item. An initiative's legitimacy and staying power are aided when formalized in policy, procedure, or measurement.

Scott's team of eighteen reside primarily in Asia, but his "virtual" team members are scattered across the globe. Although he and his team consistently deliver a quality product on time and on budget, they work long hours and suffer the loss of work-life balance. Much time is spent coordinating, aligning, and communicating to avoid or repair breakdowns in communicating across many regions, lines of business, time zones, native languages, cultures, and often competing interests.

Scott will want to advertise and secure credit for his team's successes—however small—for several reasons:

- To celebrate and build a sense of accomplishment and to avoid team burn-out or exhaustion
- To achieve a firm base of small wins to develop momentum and more success to build on
- To attract more interest and get more notice and credit, which will bring him more resources
- To get others talking about the initiative and doing the communication for him

Scott's case illustrates the four key areas of strategic positioning that must be mastered and balanced: organizational know-how, political savvy, stakeholder communication, and the ability to sustain change. Now let's take you through a personal assessment of your own strategic positioning. We'll begin with your organizational know-how.

Organizational Know-How

Organizational know-how is your knowledge of how your organization works. This includes understanding your organization from an external perspective and an internal perspective. From an external or big-picture perspective, you will want to understand what promises your organization has made to its shareholders in terms of profitability, risk, and controls. You will want to know its overall strategy—the markets it chooses to compete in and, most importantly, what factors in the business environment will positively or negatively affect its success. For example, recent global economic and environmental changes have created very strict regulations. Failure to comply with these regulations risks exposure to fines, greater oversight, damage to the brand and ultimately restricts freedom of movement. Knowing which of these regulations do and do not impact your piece of the organizational pie is important. In addition, regional unrest and instability affect costs and availability of critical resources.

From an internal perspective, you will want to understand another kind of big picture: the basics about how your organization is structured and where your unit or function fits within that structure. Equally important is knowing the predictable dilemmas, barriers, and boundaries this structure presents, which will help you plan your influence strategy. In addition, you will want to be familiar with the policies and procedures that control your decisions and what freedoms you have.

Scan Your Organizational Know-How

Circle the numbers next to those statements that you believe to be true about yourself or your team. The results of this scan will affect the kinds of goals you will set for yourself and the development activities you will choose to achieve.

1. I understand and watch the trends in the external environment that most affect our business.

2. I understand my organization's vision and values.

3. I understand the origin and rationale of my organization's strategy and structure.

4. I am aware of the predictable challenges of operating within a complex matrix structure and how these challenges might be mitigated.

5. I know how my initiative links to other initiatives on a local and global level and how my team contributes to the overall business goals.

6. I am familiar with the organizational structure and operating model of my function or business unit.

7. I know who has the formal authority and responsibility to make decisions and allocate resources related to my initiative.

8. I am familiar with the formal systems, policies, procedures, and regulatory constraints that guide decision making and resource allocation.

9. I am on the alert to opposing or countervailing forces, initiatives, or priorities (inside or outside my organization) that are likely to conflict with my initiative's priorities.

10. I know how my organization works and how to get things done within its formal structures.

Count your circles to determine your score. If your score is

8–10 You have great organizational know-how. Get out and start coaching others now.

6–7 You have moderate organizational know-how. Plan to close the gap by educating yourself in the areas you didn't circle.

0–5 Organizational know-how is an important area of development for you.

CASE STUDY
Stephen Chen and Organizational Know-How

Stephen Chen is a sales manager responsible for business development in a small but prosperous, agrarian territory in Southeast Asia. He traveled extensively and worked hard to develop business relationships and connections in his two years in this burgeoning economy. In one small business area, entrepreneurs were very eager to buy the financial products and services Stephen was offering. There was one hitch: in order to apply and qualify for these products, a business needed a landline telephone. The country was so late in getting telephone service that landlines were virtually bypassed. All of these village businesspeople had only mobile phones. Stephen presented the opportunity to his manager, who recited the company policy and told him to walk away from the business until the policy changed. Stephen was disheartened and felt he personally failed his new business contacts in the region. He was humiliated and believed he had been deceived by company rhetoric extolling the importance of innovation. Stephen had not been back into the town center, could not speak well of his company, and was losing motivation to work his territory.

With greater organizational know-how, Stephen could have avoided this situation in the first place, salvaged the innovation, and managed and even enhanced his relationships and "face" with his new business contacts. A thorough scan of the external global trends affecting his business would have alerted Stephen, his manager, and the entire sales team to understand the stringent financial regulatory trends and fraud and anti-money-laundering prevention policies and directly connect these to their world of sales. A thorough understanding of the reasons behind the current landline policy, as well as astute observation of the potential clients' access to mobile phones only, could have slowed down Stephen's sales pitch and jump-started his creative thinking about how to bring his idea to reality within this constraining environment.

Looking forward, Stephen might still be able to strategically position his idea within his organization. One important factor in delivering results in an international business environment involving multiple reporting lines and geographic regions is to have a clear line of sight from your objective to the local and global objectives of the organization.

"Line of sight" is popular business jargon borrowed from physics. Physics says that no object can be seen if no light illuminates it and travels to your eyes. In business, your job and your manager's is to draw this imaginary line between your eye and the ultimate target or object you are trying to hit. Your clear line of sight will help you know when an emerging task is tangential to or in alignment with your purpose. This should help you make decisions about what is within or out of the bounds of your assignment. Additionally, when you see an opportunity for innovation, you will know if the benefits of your innovation have a clear line of sight to the strategy and goals of your regional unit and global headquarters. This kind of understanding allows the innovator as well as the salesperson or technology expert to know how an idea or initiative fits with the corporate strategy at the local, regional, and global levels.

Stephen is flummoxed by the policy restricting financial transactions to landlines. Like any good legal contract, written policies and procedures cover every imaginable breach of boundaries, whether by carelessness or intent, in order to protect the corporation. The greater the risks of falling out of compliance with the law—in terms of damage to the corporate brand, litigation, and financial damages—the tighter the bounds of the policy. Stephen's grasp of this policy and organizational know-how may have been lost in the detail.

However, policies and procedures are also written to promote and encourage the choices and behaviors the organization expresses in its company values and guiding principles. This is where Stephen's organizational know-how will come in handy. One of the organization's guiding principles is innovation. So Stephen must reframe his sales disappointment as a setback or challenge to his innovation. The company innovation policy states that when you experience a challenge to your innovation, you should examine it and initiate a project to address the challenge.

Stephen's innovation has a line of sight to two key organizational objectives: to increase revenue and to innovate. Stephen will want to begin his homework by uncovering both the supporting policies and the challenging policies in this area. He also will want to find out who has formal authority in this area or who is most outspoken in promoting innovation and find ways to get to know and align himself with like-minded individuals and their initiatives.

This is the beginning of strategic positioning. The ability to influence across boundaries requires the motivation to maneuver within a large and complex internal and external business environment. Stephen's personal network of connections will be another essential resource in promoting his innovation.

In the meantime, Stephen will want to recover and maintain his new network of connections and relationships with the men and women who are doing business using their mobile phones. They still require financial services. What if Stephen could help them get what they need now outside his company? He would have to go out of his way and lose this round of sales, but he would gain the respect and gratitude of businesspeople in his region. They will be served, and these business relationships will be solidified. Using his personal network of connections, Stephen can seek out and uncover alternative financing for these people.

ORGANIZATIONAL KNOW-HOW
Actions, Tools, and Best Practices

Here are some ways to get smart about your organization:

- *Read your company's annual report.* It may seem dry at first, but look for an accomplishment or a challenge you are familiar with. Find your region and the product line or function you represent and read about your unit's achievements. The report will be written in the passive voice, as if things happened without anyone doing them, but knowing the backstory and the names of the team members who accomplished a challenging feat can be very motivating.

- *Seek out a handful of reliable sources to educate yourself about what is going on in your organization outside your area of responsibility and interest and in the region you serve.*

- *Select mentors with better and broader knowledge of your organization.* Employ the practice of having several mentors to ensure that you will not become overly dependent on one mentor and that you get a broad view. Ask questions and learn about your organization's big picture. Learn about your *mentors'* needs and expectations and find ways to reciprocate their efforts on your behalf. From these mentors, carefully select those reputed to be successful innovators. Learn how they *think* about innovation in a highly bureaucratic or complicated business environment. Ask them what they *did* to succeed, and learn the specifics of one story to create a positive image in your mind. Ask them how they *remained motivated* or persevered. If they do offer you advice, whether you use it or not, be sure to circle back to thank them for their story, let them know how it inspired you, and tell them the status of your own innovation.

■ *Learn about your organization through the eyes of your company's customers and shareholders.* They have interests outside your area of responsibility, so think outside-in. Identify and bookmark a handful of key competitors and track their performance. Pursue your personal professional education about the economy in general.

■ *Make connections with your organization's global marketing department to learn about the trends in your organization's key customer groups.*

■ *Reciprocate: be a mentor.* Share your insights. Teach your team about your stakeholders' interests, the organization's position in the market, and its customers.

Political Savvy

Another key component of strategically positioning your initiative is to understand how things get done *informally* within your organization. A commonly held belief in many cultures is that to be considered *political* is not a compliment. In cultures with less tolerance for ambiguity and expectations of open, direct, and transparent transactions, being overly political generally means you are self-promoting and cannot be trusted; that you are insincere, sneaky, and manipulative in your relationships; and that you "manage up" or pander to your bosses.

Political savvy, on the other hand, is a critical influence resource. To influence without formal position power and authority will require you to recognize other sources of influence and align your initiative with them. You will want to learn how to recognize and align your initiative with the weight and momentum of already-established and popular initiatives that have overcome the barriers you now face.

One of these barriers may be obscurity. In a large international organization, your idea or initiative may be lost among thousands and not enjoy the attention and recognition of those with the budgets and subject-matter experts you need to get results. Political savvy means knowing how to broaden the base of support for your initiative.

Having a broad base of support does not always include the support of a hierarchy of executives. You may find it more effective to influence them through the support of their trusted advisors or opinion leaders. At the conclusion of this book we will meet Dee, who deliberately and skillfully drove her innovation under the radar without the notice of any management other than her own solid-line manager. Dee's influence strategy was to use a broad base of support drawn from her personal professional network of regional and sector or functional subject-matter experts. Without this broad base of support, she could not have achieved her results.

Being political is about favorably positioning or promoting yourself. Having political savvy is about favorably positioning and promoting your idea or initiative by attaching it to the critical mass and momentum of already popular or important interests. The distinction is important.

Scan Your Political Savvy

Circle the numbers next to those statements that you believe to be true about yourself or your team. The results of this scan will affect the kinds of goals you will set for yourself and the development activities you will choose to achieve.

1. I can identify the key informal gatekeepers, opinion leaders, resisters, stoppers, influencers, and informal power holders in my unit.
2. I intentionally connect with and form key alliances to broaden my base of support.
3. I understand current pressures, internal competition, and competing priorities, and I know who has what to lose.

4. I take time to uncover the interests of a variety of stakeholders outside my own product or project area.

5. I encourage debate and am aware of the broad range of personal likes, dislikes, and stands—including my own—on issues of importance within my organization.

6. I join group efforts (or social networks) to exert influence on the actions of other larger entities, organizations, or groups.

7. I know now or make a habit of learning whom I can align myself with—without needing to go to the "top."

8. I actively and deliberately help others and repay favors in kind. I value the principle of exchange and reciprocity, but I do not expect others to follow my example.

9. I provide persuasive proof of the benefits of my initiative to key stakeholders.

10. I know how to get things done ethically outside formal organizational structures and procedures. I am able to efficiently circumvent barriers with the least amount of distraction and for maximum benefit.

Count your circles to determine your score. If your score is

8–10   You are extremely politically savvy. Get out and educate others now.

6–7   You are somewhat politically savvy. Plan to close the gap by educating yourself in the areas you didn't circle.

0–5   Political savvy is an important area of development for you. Examine your core beliefs about what "political" means.

CASE STUDY
Motoko Higashi and Political Savvy

Motoko Higashi is an executive of GFC, a global corporation headquartered in Hong Kong. She received unexpected on-the-job training in political savvy when she was assigned a plum position in

Paris. As you read her story, identify the lessons she learned about the art of strategic positioning through the use of political savvy.

Motoko Higashi was born and raised in Osaka, Japan. She received her doctorate in jurisprudence from Oxford and her master of business administration from INSEAD. Since coming to GFC, she has made great strides in new business development, led the global-local restructuring efforts, and for the past four years headed the emerging markets office for the Latin America region.

GFC recently reorganized its world regions into fewer, larger markets, and Motoko was appointed executive vice president of the European Region and assigned to the Paris office. She knows this four-year assignment is usually awarded to a soon-to-retire executive as his last role in GFC. Motoko is the first non-European, the first female, and the first person of color to ever hold this post.

The Paris office's reputation is as a low-profile and inactive office. For decades, the office has been little more than a travel agency and welcome center for GFC's international managers as they pass through Europe.

Motoko's manager, Isamu Bello, was searching for the most effective manager with the best track record in the field for this job. He personally selected Motoko to head this region because of her performance in every office in which she's served—and he expects her to deliver results in several key areas. One of his goals is to radically change the perception of the Paris office to that of a vibrant and essential hub of business development.

The entire GFC management team has a stake in the Paris office because so many of the corporation's influential shareholders and investors reside or have businesses in this region. This is why Isamu wanted Motoko's drive and ability to produce results in the center of the revitalization of this region. However, three native-European executives in particular, Derik, Annika, and Gunnar, coveted the new spotlight on this previously dormant region and the use of Paris as a final preretirement reward. They headed their own regional lines of business and felt strongly they could develop more new business with

European companies if they had Motoko's position, even while holding onto and developing their current territories.

At first Motoko felt this growing interest in her region meant she would be expected to report to these three business line heads; to the CEO, who frequently travels through Europe himself; and to Isamu, her solid-line manager. This was not an unusual arrangement in the corporation's global-local business model, where product line profit-and-loss (P&L) owners shared regional and functional services and reporting authority. Motoko often made light of having three business line heads to whom she reported. "And one CEO," her chief executive officer always added.

For the past ten years, Derik has been very involved in the Nordic countries and with the European Union. Motoko learned early on that although she may be responsible for all the countries in her region, the EU is like a country in and of itself and she needed Derik's institutional knowledge. Annika was ensconced in the United Kingdom and Motoko doesn't make a move on UK engagement without first talking with Annika.

Motoko said of her thinking, "The European shareholders are GFC's most influential shareholders, and some of the most powerful people on our executive committee are European. When those executives retire from the GFC, their careers will have greater links to Europe. I want access to these important people when they leave GFC, so I have to keep the long view in mind."

She quickly perceived the interest in her region was more than for information reporting. Derik, Annika, and Gunnar were positioning themselves as claimants to the European post. They were privately meeting with the CEO individually to make their case, propose their new business development solutions, and stake their claim to the relationships with the countries' capital leaders, wealthy business owners, and shareholders of the region.

Motoko said, "Someone implied that my partner was in Tokyo and that I would want to return there very shortly and therefore did not have the long-term commitment this regional turnaround required.

Fortunately, the head of HR came to me personally to confirm these rumors about my plans for my future, so I had an opportunity to learn of this deliberate smear campaign and head it off."

Her participation as a subject-matter expert in world forums, prestigious university panels, and local community activities throughout her career has created a wide and strong public face for Motoko and a strong network of support inside and outside her organization. She soon learned from multiple sources that Derik was waging what they characterized as a full-scale coup to strip her of any substantive role in Europe.

She put it this way, "Derik and Annika and Gunnar collectively and independently started to stage a coup. Derik wanted control of Europe, and the CEO initially approved. Derik tried to reorganize our European operations by taking the core functional and substantive business relationships and leaving what he called the 'soft' functions, HR and office administration, to me. But I am not totally naïve. I am not just going to lie down, give up, and go away. I learned in my last post in a regional office that I do not have to react quickly and assertively. I can smile and appear compliant. But behind my outward appearance, my fight is there."

She went to the CEO in Hong Kong and made him aware that she had heard the rumors about her lack of commitment. She pledged to deliver the aggressive goals set for her and vowed she and her team would be in Europe for the full four years. She presented an ambitious strategy and a quick restructuring for her region. The CEO was thoroughly persuaded by Motoko's insights and the quick results she had already delivered. He distributed her plan personally at his next executive committee, and it was approved without discussion.

Motoko shared her thoughts on the need for political savvy, which she is just now beginning to fully employ. "You need political savvy the more senior you become and the more international the organization is. In the best global organizations, we cherry-pick very, very bright people who are very good at what they do. However, the more senior you get, the fewer opportunities for advancement there are, and everyone is vying for a few coveted spots. Everyone wants to be recognized within what turns out to be a very small world."

Motoko's ability to deliver results has never been from an individualistic perspective, and she knows she will not be able to succeed without collective support. "I need everyone on the executive team and on my team because I have a large region I must serve and derive profits from. I need to use the executive team's networks, but I also need to let them know I own ultimate accountability for results in my region. I am not daunted by this responsibility. I am entirely capable of delivering results."

She went on to explain the influence strategies she uses with different individuals. "Annika and I have a slightly better relationship. I extend favors to her when I have the power to do so. I freely let her know if I learn of something particularly relevant to her region or position. I am more careful with Derrick, but I do occasionally tell him something I think he should know about. I'm not an information hoarder."

Motoko feels her eyes have been opened in a new way through this experience. "Unfortunately, my peers are not forthright in sharing their agendas. So now I listen to what they say within the much broader perspective of personal agendas. I have become more politically savvy. I am more careful where I tell the truth: I tell Isamu the truth."

She learned another tough lesson. She realized that like anyone else, her CEO can be influenced by the person he sees and speaks to most often or has seen most recently. She works on the assumption that his commitment could last only as long as it takes for the next person to present an alternative and compelling case. Because she is not situated in corporate headquarters with regular face-to-face, down-the-hall connection to the CEO, she works through his other trusted advisors to influence him. She and Isamu have created a schedule to keep in touch with the CEO and his opinion leaders very regularly, she said, "so that he is intimately familiar with our voices and the status of our efforts."

This experience has also helped Motoko to articulate her personal values and standards for delivering results. "I will always be trustworthy and loyal to those whom I trust, but I will not need to tell everyone the unvarnished truth. This does not mean I will lie; I will just not need to be forthright with everyone. I think one of the reasons the CEO has such high regard for me, besides the fact that I deliver results, is that I am forthright with him."

As for delivering results, Motoko is delivering them. "Our European shareholders are pleased with the attention we give them. They represent over 20 percent of our total company revenue and appear happy to have someone who is non-European cover the entire region. In less than two years, all of our countries, all of our shareholders know us. The increased budget I won back has allowed us to place coordinators to cover every country. Before, these shareholders really didn't know GFC well and never felt truly aligned with us. Now they are volunteering to host regional forums to discuss economic recovery with us. They have certain items they want to put on the agenda and to achieve. It is not my plan; it is their plan."

Motoko's story illustrates several of the resources required to influence the outcome by favorably positioning her initiative in a very competitive internal setting. One of the most important points to keep in mind is that Motoko would not have been effective if she had not been strategic in delivering results. Her past reputation for achieving challenging goals; her scan of the opportunities and threats in the external and internal environments; her initial focus on short-term, high-impact, low-effort opportunities her team won immediately; and her four-year strategy and implementation of a new regional structure positioned members of her team with powerful stakeholders in each country capital. All these results provided a strong business case and support base to fend off internal threats.

POLITICAL SAVVY
Actions, Tools, and Best Practices

Based on your initial scan of your political savvy earlier in this chapter and on Motoko's experience, what do you need to do to develop this resource? Select from among the best practices below to improve your strategic positioning by using your political know-how.

■ *Identify a successful innovation or initiative and investigate how it was executed.* Call the project executive or key team members. Ask them if they might identify one lesson they learned in getting work done through the informal channels of your organization. Share your idea and ask how it might be accomplished outside formal avenues.

■ *Identify and emulate your politically savvy role models.* Identify those you admire who are politically savvy (not "political"). Imagine how they would behave in a politically sensitive or opportune moment and act as if they are there to guide you.

■ *Enlarge your base of support.* Identify the opinion leaders among decision makers you hope to influence. Whom do the decision makers turn to? Win the support of opinion leaders at the lowest level possible without going to the busiest and most unavailable person at the top. These are people with information about or access to funding or who are proven implementers. Find out what they need and do what you can to provide it. Learn about your stakeholders' personal interests and uncover mutual interests.

■ *Find others who are willing to let your successes be known.* Your past performance will signal the promise of your current initiatives—if people know about you. As we've seen with Motoko, doing a good job is not enough. You have to have a solid base of support that is aware of your achievements.

■ *Solidify your business case.* Prepare to present persuasive evidence to sell the problems and the opportunities your innovation or initiative is designed to resolve.

■ *Before you sell your business case, identify those who designed, originated, or have a stake in the status quo or the problem you are responsible for addressing.* Investigate to understand the rationale behind the original design so you are sensitive to the history of your assignment or initiative. From this perspective of appreciation, prepare to sell the potential costs of business as usual, sell the opportunities in its resolution, and identify the group of people whose collective influence you need.

Stakeholder Communication

The purpose of stakeholder communication is to develop support and momentum while keeping stakeholders informed. The most basic purpose of stakeholder communication is to build support—resources, commitment, and momentum—and to anticipate and overcome objections.

Scan Your Stakeholder Communication

Circle the numbers next to those statements that you believe to be true about yourself or your team. The results of this scan will affect the kinds of goals you will set for yourself and the development activities you will choose to achieve.

1. I have an up-to-date list of all those who have an interest in, who may benefit from, or who may thwart the success of my initiative.
2. I form relationships with others who deal directly with my key stakeholders to learn information regarding their interests.
3. I emphasize the benefits of my initiative to key stakeholders from the personal, group, and organizational levels.
4. I willingly "overcommunicate." I allocate much time to coordinating, aligning, and communicating with various stakeholders.
5. I am aware of communication-related problems inherent in the matrix organization's multiple reporting structure. I anticipate and preempt these breakdowns.
6. I find other advocates who will communicate about and promote my initiative so that key stakeholders will hear reinforcing favorable reports by others.

7. I have a stakeholder recovery plan to implement if I have allowed a stakeholder to fall through the cracks.

8. I conduct regular biweekly or monthly calls to listen to and inform my stakeholders about my initiative.

9. I have a minimal and memorable "elevator" message tailored to appeal to the interests of and capture the attention of each of my busy stakeholders.

10. I deliberately gain the support of key stakeholders to create a critical mass of support for the change my initiative requires.

Count your circles to determine your score. If your score is

8–10　You are an extremely effective stakeholder communicator. Support your peers and teammates by sharing your best practices with them.

6–7　You are a somewhat effective communicator. Plan to close the gap by targeting some of the actions you didn't circle.

0–5　Stakeholder communication is an important area of development for you. Analyze the cause of your limited communication. What is the cost you are paying for not staying in better contact with your stakeholders?

CASE STUDY
Roberta Juliano and Stakeholder Communication

After the first six months in her most important global assignment, Roberta Juliano was not getting the cooperation she needed to move her initiative forward. The senior managers in her organization whose support she needed did not pay attention to her initiative. Because they ignored her initiative, the subject-matter experts who reported to them were able to ignore her as well. So the people whose time and support she required—her lateral or peer dependencies—did not fulfill their portion of their assignments that overlapped hers. Even though President Wong personally commissioned her initiative,

Roberta patently refused to continually refer to his authority by saying "But President Wong says . . ." She believed that the more she used President Wong's position authority, the more it would diminish her own authority and credibility. Neither would she report others to President Wong or attempt to shame them publicly.

As Roberta put it, "I want them all to collaborate with me. The last place I want to go is through President Wong. At times you may need to drop a name. But I hate it when people say 'I expect this would be President Wong's response' or 'President Wong said this.'"

Because of her past successes, Roberta has a strong belief in herself. She believes cooperation will come when people make the connection between her initiative and their interests and accountabilities. She keeps the long view in mind, but she is impatient for results.

Roberta decided her initiative needed greater visibility and started doing some public relations and advertising work of her own. She started the *Global Transformation Newsletter* to publish all achievements no matter how small. The first few small wins, Roberta reasoned, would eventually turn into many small wins and bit by bit create an avalanche of momentum in her favor. Whenever a better-known project leader collaborated with her or demonstrated the usefulness of her transformation services team, she gave that leader's initiative a headline in her newsletter. She sent her newsletter to President Wong and to each of his senior managers and their various chains of influence.

Roberta stated, "My newsletter is creating interest and motivation for the other senior managers to get in line with my program. I highlight the successes. People want to be on the list of those who are doing the right thing. It's a kind of peer pressure. I won't put my stakeholders at odds with each other, so I have to know what might put them at odds."

Roberta's newsletter provides a vehicle to ensure she regularly communicates with and updates her stakeholders. This helps her sustain momentum and change by creating a regular institutionally recognized communiqué. Her action also demonstrates her political savvy because she is using the power of the group to enlarge her base of support. By creatively using the newsletter, she carefully avoids stepping on any toes in keeping with her commitment to sustainable, trusting relationships and collaboration.

Let's use Roberta's example to illustrate the three steps to making stakeholder communication an effective habit.

Effective Stakeholder Communication

Each contact with your stakeholders should begin with a clear sense of purpose. What are you trying to communicate? From this base, effective stakeholder communication has three steps:

- *Create awareness:* Begin with information sharing. You do not want your stakeholders to be caught unawares or hear about your initiative from a negatively biased perspective. Create awareness of your initiative, idea, or issue by clearly and concisely informing key stakeholders and those who deal directly with these stakeholders. Establish a regular process—a monthly e-mail report or newsletter, like Roberta did.

- *Promote understanding and relevance:* When your stakeholders are well informed about your initiative, the next question is, "How do I connect the importance of my initiative with the priorities of my stakeholders?" Know the various initiatives and interests of your stakeholders and bring your initiative alive by answering this question for each of them. Provide specific examples to illustrate how your initiative connects with and is relevant to your stakeholders' goals. By including the stakeholders' activities in her newsletter, Roberta drew a direct link between her initiatives and theirs.

- *Motivate ownership and action:* When your stakeholders understand and connect with your initiative in a sufficiently compelling manner, the next question is, "What specifically do I need my stakeholders to do?" When your initiative requires the active participation of your stakeholders, be prepared to ask for what you need. Your job is to provide a clear statement of need, provide proof of that need, propose a specific course of action, and offer clarity about immediate first steps. Roberta motivated her stakeholders using a peripheral influence tool we'll cover in chapter 3 called "social proof." It's the same as peer pressure. Roberta was savvy enough to know her stakeholders did not want to be the only one who was not on board in a publication their CEO was sure to see.

STAKEHOLDER COMMUNICATION
Actions, Tools, and Best Practices

So far we've looked at three different approaches to communicating with stakeholders. In the example above, Roberta used a newsletter targeted exclusively at communicating with her stakeholders—and used her political savvy to influence reluctant supporters through peer pressure. Motoko and her manager, Isamu, committed to a schedule of telephone, e-mail, and face-to-face contacts with the CEO to influence his ongoing support and put their voices and accomplishments in front of him when they could not be there physically—disadvantaged by their region being on the other side of the world. In our first example, Scott planned to recover two stakeholders who felt neglected by setting up a calendar of regular meetings to brief them.

Here are some ways to influence your stakeholders through close communication:

- *Refresh your list of internal stakeholders with your team.* List anyone who has a direct or indirect stake in your initiative, who benefits from or has an interest in your initiative, or who may bring pressure to bear on resources and decisions.

- *Identify your external stakeholders, the ultimate beneficiaries whose programs or initiatives align with yours.* Identify ways in which you will "listen" to them and have a balanced and broad perspective of their views.

- *Recover neglected stakeholders and deliberately overcommunicate.* Identify key stakeholders who could be better informed. Write a letter confessing your past neglect and your commitment to be more proactive going forward. Remind your stakeholders of the value of your initiative and how it supports their programs, projects, and interests. Ask your stakeholders to reconfirm what they need and expect from you and your team. Set up a systematic approach to honor your commitment to keep in touch consistently and personally in the way they prefer. Use your e-mail's calendar function to schedule regular meetings, telephone calls, or e-mail communiqués.

■ *Be on the alert for accomplishments and achievements of your stakeholders, and send stakeholders notes of recognition and appreciation.*

■ *Create a minimal and memorable message, a simple, easy-to-remember theme that requires minimal explanation.* Summarize your initiative and communicate it in a way that captures interest and makes it easier for your stakeholders to repeat. This will leverage your stakeholders as people who can sell your initiative for you.

How to Create Your Minimal and Memorable Message

Before you create your message of influence tailored to each individual stakeholder, you will want to prepare yourself in three important ways. First, you will want to know your audience. Listen carefully to what your stakeholders say about themselves and their self-interests, and listen to what others say about your stakeholders' styles, reputations, and personal preferences. Second, prepare to adjust your content, language, and style based on what you've learned about them. Third, plan to appeal to your stakeholders' self-interests.

Once you complete your preliminary homework about each stakeholder, you need to create three basic components of a minimal and memorable message: your claim, evidence to support your claim, and the specific value your initiative provides your listener.

■ *Claim:* What is the business problem or opportunity your initiative addresses?

■ *Evidence:* What is a specific story that offers an example of a recent success and the results you and your team have recently achieved?

- *Value:* What is your initiative's value or benefit to this stake-holder? Think, "What's in it for me?" (WIIFM) from your stake-holder's perspective.

It helps to rehearse your message aloud to make sure you have a minimal and memorable message and not a history of the modern world. Time yourself. Your message should last no more than thirty to sixty seconds. Ask yourself these questions or ask a colleague to look for the following criteria:

- *Clear:* Do you speak plainly and avoid jargon?
- *Concise:* Have you kept your message short and simple?
- *Compelling:* Have you provided a story or example that illus-trates your message and makes it come alive in the mind of your listener?
- *Commercial:* Have you clearly stated the value for this audience?

Remember, the purpose of a minimal and memorable message is to provide your audience with a message that can be consistently repeated and tailored to different stakeholders.

The Ability to Sustain Change

The ability to sustain change is essential to strategically position-ing your idea or initiative within an organization for the long run. Sustainability means your initiative will endure for future generations without burdening those future generations. It means your initiative is more than a temporarily popular idea. To build sustainability, not only must you plan your initiative's initial resource and infrastructure support, you must also account for its future legitimacy within the future direction of the organization, future sources of funding, and internal organizational supporting mechanisms.

Scan Your Ability to Sustain Change

Circle the numbers next to those statements that you believe to be true about yourself or your team. The results of this scan will affect the kinds of goals you will set for yourself and the development activities you will choose to achieve.

1. I know the basic tenets of building sustainability and organizational development.

2. I use existing formal organizational support mechanisms or systems (e.g., terminology, financial systems, human resource policies or position descriptions, reporting procedures) to reinforce the legitimacy of my initiative or idea.

3. I build into my initiative the necessary technical assistance and training for developing the new competencies and skills it requires.

4. I ensure future funding by creating a formal budget with income sources sufficient to cover the expenses of my initiative.

5. I seek to build the momentum and stability of my idea or initiative by aligning it with other established popular ideas or initiatives.

6. I plan for, achieve, advertise, and reward small wins to create momentum and attract the commitment and cooperation of others.

7. I flexibly adjust my plans and personal ownership to accommodate and involve others who want ownership of and input to my initiative.

8. As more people are attracted to my initiative, I am able to let go of and share ownership and credit for the success of my initiative.

9. I am able to adapt with minimum frustration to the slower decision making that occurs as more people need to be involved in the decision-making process.

10. I reinforce the desired behaviors necessary to sustain momentum for my initiative by linking them to formal rewards.

Count your circles to determine your score. If your score is

8–10　You are extremely effective in sustaining change. Not everyone understands this, so tactfully coach your team and peers by asking them where sustaining change is included in their plans.

6–7　You are somewhat effective at sustaining change. Plan to close the gap by targeting some of the actions you didn't circle.

0–5　Sustaining change is an important area of development for you. Your initiative may be short-lived if it is not stabilized through formal organizational systems, policies, and procedures.

THE ABILITY TO SUSTAIN CHANGE
Actions, Tools, and Best Practices

As we saw from Motoko's situation, she not only fended off claimants to her new European post, she established a foothold for long-term, sustainable changes in her region by achieving a number of quick wins. Scott Farris formally included his strategy work into his and his team's balanced scorecards and identified the rater to entrench this assignment in the formal performance rating system. Roberta Juliano instituted a newsletter as a regular communication vehicle to publicly advertise the achievements of those who cooperate with her. Listed below are other actions, tools, and best practices you can use to institutionalize change for the future.[1]

- *Build momentum with small accomplishments.* Accumulate good will by sharing credit for early accomplishments to establish a foothold and advertise. Plan to achieve, report, celebrate, and promote even the smallest accomplishments early. Look back and identify any small wins you have already accomplished and report them in a team newsletter. Widely advertise early successes.

- *Stabilize and institutionalize your initiative by building formal supporting mechanisms quickly.* Ask one of your managers to confirm that your initiative is formally accounted for in his or her budget. Write up a formal job description for any new project personnel, part-time or full-time, and send it to HR so that it is a recognized position. Formalize an assignment by sending out an announcement in your business newsletter or on your internal Facebook equivalent. Encourage the individual who has the formalized assignment to post it on his or her external professional social network (such as LinkedIn).

- *Be sure to accept credit and recognition whenever possible and give credit and recognition where it is due.* More resources, challenging assignments, and opportunities will be given to those who are recognized for achievement. This is the sociological finding often referred to as the "Matthew effect"—the rich get richer and the poor get poorer—based on biblical scripture that states, "For all those who have, more will be given."[2] Try to secure appropriate credit and exposure whenever possible. For example, promote your team or sponsor to others within your organization. Determine with whom you might share credit for your work or idea. Be creative: identify ways in which others can advertise your work. Anticipate how to avoid allowing your idea to be unintentionally hijacked by someone more outspoken. Reexamine your behaviors or patterns that inadvertently give your ideas away.

- *Create rituals, fun awards ceremonies, small incentives, and imaginative bonuses to reward and recognize achievement.* You can invite other teams to join in your team's celebration and share the celebratory cake. As much as possible, create the identity of your team as a cohesive unit whose time and talents are recognized and directed to the same initiative.

- *Write up the procedure that describes the best practices you discovered in the process of delivering your initiative.* Include a statement of the lessons learned. If there is a community of practice—subject-matter experts formally or informally convening or networked to address the problem or opportunity your initiative is concerned with—offer to post your procedure and lessons learned on that community's website. If your initiative is related to the roles and responsibilities of a Center of Excellence (COE), offer to present your results and methodology at the COE's next best-practice forum. Give your process or methodology a name. This will relieve others from having to reinvent the wheel, help advertise and sustain your team's results, and propel forward momentum.

- *Start presenting and speaking about your initiative as a form of advertisement.* Scan the wider organization to identify other complementary programs and ideas; align your idea to another view or strategically important rising-star project. Get your idea on the agendas of these complementary programs and prepare a ten-minute presentation of your results, findings, and best practices.

Leveraging Organizational Interests and Line of Sight

As we've discussed thus far, the critical foundation for delivering results in a complex international organization is to favorably and strategically position your initiative within the organization. Use the scan below as a reminder of the assessment you will want to make to confirm the legitimacy of your initiative within the organization.

Scan Your Initiative's Strategic Position

As a final assessment of your initiative's overall strategic position, circle the numbers next to those statements below that you believe to be true about your initiative. The results of this scan will help you to confirm the strategic position and legitimacy of your initiative within the organization.

1. The initiative supports and furthers the purpose, stated values, guiding principles, corporate social responsibilities, and overall reason for being or mission of the organization.

2. Investment in the initiative supports the future vision of the organization because it aligns with the long-term viability, innovation, and evolution of the company.

3. The initiative is aligned with the company's overall strategy and with other projects of strategic priority and has a direct line of sight to the success of the business.

4. The initiative positively impacts overall profitability through efficiency savings; directly or indirectly increases funding, sales, and income generation; does not risk exposing the company to loss, adverse publicity, or damage to its brand; and is in compliance with governing regulations.

5. The initiative's strategy includes systematic two-way communication with key stakeholders and the use of connections to influential networks to gain access to important information and opportunities.

6. The initiative has sufficient support from opinion leaders and sponsorship from senior managers with resources.

7. The initiative is structured to sustain itself year over year through self-funding, minimization of expenses, and maintenance of operating capacity and customer service.

8. The initiative's strategy includes systematic communication with consumers and organizations outside the company to stay abreast of external trends that may impact the company and the initiative.

9. The initiative's strategy includes systematic communication and engagement activities with employees connected with the initiative to improve the experience, satisfaction, and engagement indicators that are part of the business plan.

10. The initiative uses economies of scale and is planned to be applied to other regions, businesses, commercial markets, products, or services.

Count your circles to determine your score. If your score is

8–10   Your initiative is well positioned strategically. Congratulations. You have a solid basis from which to begin your next steps in influencing across boundaries. Coach others in the art of strategic positioning.

6–7   Your initiative is relatively well positioned strategically. Plan to close the gap by targeting some of the items you didn't circle. Begin to plot your steppingstone strategy (below).

0–5   Strategic positioning of your initiative is an important area of development for you. Begin by plotting a steppingstone strategy to systematically and strategically build the support you need. Your ability to influence others to drive the results of your initiative may be lacking this firm foundation. Highlight the items you did not circle; review the actions, tools, and best practices lists; and make strategic positioning a priority in your goal setting.

Plot Your Strategic Positioning Steppingstone Strategy

Now that you are familiar with all the elements of strategic positioning, you will want to create a plan to influence the outcome by favorably positioning your initiative within the organization. Using a "steppingstone strategy" means you understand that this favorable positioning requires multiple moves. Whether you are playing a quick game of checkers or a more deliberate game of chess, you may make one move at a time while having multiple pieces on the board. Using an image of a checkerboard or chessboard will help you conceptualize the idea of seeing the entire board—or organizational environment in which you will be operating—at once. Creating a steppingstone strategy to influence others across the board begins with having your many resources lined up at the starting position and a firm understanding of the obstacles or boundaries you will encounter and will have to cross along the way to a successful finish. Each move represents a new influence challenge. Several of your pieces or resources will be in play at the same time—some lateral, some forward, some backward—and you will always want to see where you have deployed your resources.

Begin by writing down the ultimate position or finish line you believe your initiative must occupy within the overall strategy and structure of the organization. Then fill in your starting place relative to that future outcome. The empty squares between you and the goal represent the various gaps, boundaries, or influence challenges you will address in your journey across the board.

Look ahead to the steps you anticipate and the key players you will want to influence. What is each step's goal? What action do you expect to take and what outcome do you hope to achieve? Where do you expect to spend time laterally, influencing peers? Where do you expect you must learn the current organizational strategy and system-wide politics, policies, and procedures that may work for or against your initiative?

As we defined "boundaries" in the introduction of this book, any-thing that inhibits performance, any hurdle, challenge, or dilemma you will have to address and resolve to close a performance gap is yours to identify and cross. We differentiated barriers that are internal to the individual performer and barriers that are external to the per-former, that is, an organizational policy, procedure, system, practice, or element of its culture that is the source of the gap in performance. As you progress in your thinking and planning to strategically posi-tion your initiative, it is important to recognize the difference between the boundaries that are within your control as an individual to cross and those you will need to collaborate with others to confront. Below is a list of actions, tools, and best practices you can employ to improve your strategic positioning.

STRATEGIC POSITIONING
Actions, Tools, and Best Practices

Now is your chance to integrate the four elements of strategic posi-tioning into a list of actions you can take to develop this important resource. In the conclusion of this book, we will study the case of a successful international manager who depends on her strategic position throughout the course of delivering her innovation.

- *Present a clear, concise, and memorable statement of strategy.* First and foremost, and if you do nothing else on the list below, present your organizational strategy in terms your audience understands. Make it short and sweet. Avoid a lot of jargon. Avoid pages upon pages. If you can't say it in less than five minutes and in two to three slides, you aren't ready to present it. Make the connection between the strategy and your listeners' daily jobs using terms like "This means, when you . . . " Allow time for questions and answer them in terms your listeners understand and appreciate.

- *Learn just how much organizational know-how your peers and team members have.* Plan to "meet your audience where they are" to discuss the business strategy in terms you've learned this audience understands.

- *Uncover rumors and gossip.* Respectfully and sincerely ask your team, peers, and other audiences to share some of the current rumors and gossip they are hearing about the organization. Then systematically, patiently, and truthfully address the individual items. If a subject is off-limits, explain why. Acknowledge any recurring themes (confusion, optimism, fear, sense of readiness) without shame or blame and address them as candidly as possible. A lot of truth and a lot of fiction are circulating in your organization. Help people know the difference. Assume you are not as informed as you think you are. Ask. Listen. In the more indirect cultures, you may ask people to write down what they believe *others* might misunderstand. As we will discuss in chapter 3, for individuals raised in cultures that may consider it disrespectful to speak so plainly or to appear to complain and that respect and defer to status and hierarchy, you may need to appeal to their sense of collective well-being and your desire to serve the greater good through this knowledge. In some cultures you can be direct and to the point. In other cultures you will want to diplomatically and subtly convey your interest in learning more about the emotional climate that often shows up in the rumors and gossip. When you understand your audience, your personal credibility, authenticity, approachability, and authority will be much improved.

- *Plan to educate each audience.* Treat your audience like business professionals who are attending business school. Meet them at their level of understanding and work up from there. What specific examples about their current and anticipated future local business environment can you use to illustrate why the strategy is shaped as it is?

- *Facilitate an internal and external organizational "big picture scan" with your team.* (See appendix A for a complete description of this process.) The outcome of a scan of the big picture in which you and your team will deliver results is threefold. First, you and your team will identify the systemic boundaries that will need to be addressed and crossed in order to be successful, collectively pinpointing the factors that are most likely to push and pull your organization as a whole and your areas of responsibility in particular. Second, this big picture scan answers the question "why?"—the business case or rationale for change. Knowing why helps mitigate the sense of feeling like part of a moving target. Knowing your organization's drivers improves your organizational know-how. Finally, and perhaps most important in regard to influence, facilitating a scan engages your team in strategic critical thinking to build a foundation of shared understanding and personal meaning. We'll learn later in this book why engaging your cognition or rational thinking is one essential route to persuasion and to creating enduring commitment to a decision.

  The unique characteristics of the competitive international business landscape in which you want to succeed require routine scanning. Change in one element of the environment can cause a ripple effect of consequences in other related areas.

Success in strategically positioning your idea or initiative means you have favorably influenced the setting in which your initiative will be delivered. Like entrepreneurs who bring their new ideas, products, and services into a vast market, you must prove your initiative belongs and has staying power. With your initiative strategically positioned within your complex international organization—no small task—the other influence resources can be planted in fertile soil.

The next resource, cross-cultural know-how, is another fundamental influence resource in the international business environment. As we've discussed thus far, the ability to influence the attitudes and behaviors of people from all cultures toward a goal without formal authority requires cultural intelligence, a firm understanding of the dimensions of cultures, and the ability to communicate across cultures.

Two

Building Your Cross-Cultural Know-How

This chapter makes the business case for the critical importance of your cultural intelligence, or CQ, and your ability to know when and how to adjust mentally, emotionally, and physically to dimensions of culture and to communicate effectively across cultures. The goal is to help you find ways to communicate so that you include and can be understood by people of different cultures and native languages, recognizing, affirming, and valuing the worth of individuals. You will find pragmatic cross-cultural communication tools you can begin to apply immediately. You will gain self-awareness about your ability to be understood and to include people of other cultures and native languages. And you will be motivated to create a personal professional development plan to increase your cultural intelligence.

This chapter touches on three areas of cross-cultural know-how—cultural intelligence as the overarching big picture, then a closer view of the different dimensions of culture that you will want to be on the lookout for and adjust to in all of your international encounters, and then finally a very pragmatic and specific skill to use in your everyday business with people of different cultures—cross-cultural communication.

As we have discussed thus far, influence happens outside the formal authority and status assigned to managers in the organization's hierarchy. Leaders authorize themselves to influence others and are authorized by others who come to identify them as leaders.

To win the commitment and cooperation of others across cultures is challenging because of the differing attitudes toward and expectations of those with the power, authority, and status a formal title conveys. Cultures have different values, norms, and beliefs about how influence should be exerted—with authority and without it. They also differ on how decisions and transactions should be made in the context of relationships, how conflict should be managed, and how personal relationships and connections are formed.

Big Picture Scan

Before you read on, please take a moment to answer these questions.

- Do you have extended interactions with one or more members of another culture—for business or socially?

- Do you expect to be in contact with members of another culture soon?

- Are your interactions with members of other cultures of relatively short duration but is the business of high importance?

- Do you conduct business over the phone or correspond in writing with members of other cultures?

- Could a failure to handle a situation well with members of other cultures mean the loss of business, time, resources, or important relationships?

All these situations require cross-cultural know-how. Add cultural intelligence to your other intelligences, learn the dimensions of culture—yours and others'—and begin to speak more comprehensibly, and you will be better equipped to influence across boundaries.

What Is Culture?

Researchers have a wide variety of ways of looking at and defining the culture of a group of people. Definitions of culture typically include values, standards, or norms of behavior as well as rituals, beliefs, and habits of thinking. A cultural group has a shared system of communication and language, a shared history, and a shared set of assumptions about how to succeed, fail, adapt, and survive.

For the purposes of this discussion, culture consists of the *values, norms, beliefs, and rituals* of a group. The culture of a large group may include subsets with their own subcultures.

Cultural Intelligence

Cultural intelligence is your ability to adapt effectively to new cultural environments. This measure of intelligence is holistic and includes the three components of mind, body, and spirit: your cognition (your mind or the way you think), your motivation (your spirit), and your verbal and nonverbal physical adjustments (your body).[1] Cultural intelligence includes the way you plan and prepare mentally to enter into a new culture and the way you process information in the moment while you are in a new culture. It depends on how willing and motivated you are to adapt the way you think and act as well as your level of confidence that you will be effective in adapting. Your cultural intelligence also includes your ability to adjust what you look like, what you sound like, and what you say when you cross into another culture. Together, these three elements of cultural intelligence—your mind, body, and spirit—provide a clear way to build this critical resource to influencing across boundaries.

Cognitive Cultural Intelligence

Improving your cultural intelligence requires improving your thinking and teaching yourself how to think on the fly. Culture has been compared to the "software" of the mind.[2] Growing up within or prolonged exposure to a culture creates a set of programming for people within a group, a region, or a nation.[3] When you enter into a new and unfamiliar cultural environment, you enter into a group of people who have been programmed differently than you. Their thinking patterns and mind-sets may be different from yours. Using your cognitive cultural intelligence means thinking about how these differences might play out before you interact with people from another culture. You plan how you will relate to them before you meet them.

The "mind" element of your cultural intelligence also includes your ability to understand your impulses to think and act as if on automatic pilot. To be effective, you will need to avoid or override your habitual automatic responses. This means you will have to be intentionally self-conscious. For some, this level of self-awareness and self-correction can feel painful and unfamiliar. Awareness of your personal hard-wiring and the deliberate overriding of such programming require mental training.

I have found that learning in advance what preconceived notions or stereotypes people of another culture have about my personal demographics and culture is very useful. For example, people in Nordic countries who are raised to act with and expect modesty and quiet socially oriented, cooperative behavior may negatively anticipate an American businesswoman to be loud and assertive, drawing attention to herself rather than the team. When working with or traveling in Sweden or Norway, I can anticipate how I might be perceived or misunderstood if I get caught in the act of playing out this stereotype. I must plan in advance to be on the alert for cues that I am being overly loud, direct, or familiar. If I find myself about to interrupt another out of what I would consider enthusiasm for the topic but another perceives as rudeness, I can politely wait my turn to speak. I can be prepared to tone down my familiarity with the more senior managers I know well. I will be sure to not act overly familiar with the most senior delegate in the meeting. When emphasizing results, I can balance my performance-oriented remarks with my concerns for quality-of-life issues the Nordic cultures value. If I were to slip up, I would have a recovery plan in mind.

Another way to use your brain in advance of a cultural encounter is to start by being aware of what you think something means. For example, if everyone stands when you enter the room, what does that mean in your culture? What does it mean in this other culture? Does this mean that you are of a higher rank than anyone else in the room? If you are a woman, is this courtesy extended only to women? Or have you broken into a meeting you should have waited to be invited into and affronted the meeting delegates?

To be aware of what you are thinking while you are thinking it means you will have to be self-conscious and process information in the moment. For example, while someone is speaking, you have to think, "Do this other person's words and behaviors mean the same thing they might mean in my home culture?"

So developing your cognitive cultural intelligence is a matter of training your mind rather than merely filling your head with facts about the new culture you expect to come in contact with. It's learning as you go. Training your mind is about managing your own learning in new cultural environments.

But wait. What if the way you've always thought, your intellectual horsepower, is exactly what's led to your success thus far? Your past successes have reinforced your thinking and created an intuition you've come to trust and rely on. Why would you want to meddle with a good thing?

This is a very good question.

You will have to be very motivated to engage in what has just been described as rigorous relearning that involves painful self-consciousness and risks changing a winning formula. This is why your motivation to really put your heart and spirit into this new endeavor is another important element of cultural intelligence.

Motivational Cultural Intelligence

Breaking into a new culture may feel just like that—breaking a lot of plates, stepping on a lot of toes, making a lot of false starts. As you might imagine, research has shown that people do make many mistakes when they first encounter another culture. They receive negative feedback or gentle corrections before they receive any positive feedback about their efforts.[4] This requires a spirit of resilience—the determination and desire to pick yourself up and try again.

Motivational cultural intelligence refers to your personal drive and confidence in your ability to overcome the inevitable obstacles and setbacks you will encounter when trying to adapt to a new culture.

Consider it your spirit of adventure. The need to think about how you think may feel awkward and daunting and the payoff may seem too small. But if you are busy beating yourself up for one misstep, you are likely to take your head out of the game and miss the next cultural cue. This means you have to be really self-motivated and familiar with delayed gratification. Your payoff will come, but not immediately. People tend to avoid tasks and situations they believe exceed their capabilities. We seek to minimize pain and maximize pleasure. Knowing failure is ahead is usually enough of an excuse to opt out.

Belief in your ability to succeed in spite of difficulty and setbacks is called "self-efficacy." The greater your self-efficacy, the greater your motivation to persevere in the face of failures in new situations. This is the emotional and motivational heart of cultural intelligence. In spite of potential embarrassments and an initial lack of finesse, you are certain you will be able to adapt eventually to the different behaviors, rituals, and lifestyle of an unfamiliar culture. You know you will be able to build trusting relationships with and influence people whose cultural backgrounds are different from yours. A colleague from Argentina, Theresa, said her mother told her she will be able to make friends anywhere she travels as long as she smiles. Theresa is determined to smile and work at a relationship until she can get the other person to smile back. She believes, as her mother taught her, that if she begins with the relationship, any conflicts or disagreements can be managed from there.

One enemy of adapting to new cultures is your attachment to being consistent in being the person you have always been. This attachment to being who you have always been, you may say, is being authentic, and any behavior outside of your what-you-see-is-what-you-get persona would be inauthentic. People who vow to be themselves at all costs are more likely to surround themselves with others who are just like them. They are more likely to isolate themselves in the company of others from the same culture. The higher your need for consistency, the more likely you are to resist adapting to a culture with different values, norms, and beliefs. An unwillingness to see yourself adopting the mannerisms, habits, or mind-set of a different culture will severely limit your ability to make the physical adjustments necessary to be effective.

For example, I recently worked with a very successful executive who believed her personal values and beliefs were in direct opposition to those of the business culture in which she was working. She believed her organization's culture was quickly evolving into a more risk-averse, command-and-control climate. Because she wanted to be consistent, she believed she could not be true to herself in this environment. She did make an amazing turnaround once she changed her perspective and saw the organization as a culture. Her shift in perspective helped her see she was not losing or jeopardizing her true self and core values. She had no desire to change her colleagues and no worries that they would fundamentally change her authentic self. Her challenge changed from whether she would become a different person to whether she could temporarily flex her cross-cultural intelligence when she came to work. She realized she had the thinking skills, strong sense of self and motivation, and physical acumen to meet her colleagues where they were.

Physical Cultural Intelligence

Your ability to adjust your body language and adopt the habits and mannerisms of others is your physical CQ. If you are extremely resistant—if your mind is definitely not in the game—then you may well be unable to adopt some of the behaviors an encounter with a different culture may require. People with high physical cultural intelligence are able to alter their tone of voice, expression, eye contact, and posture for the convenience or comfort of a person from another culture. Physical adjustment in what you look like, sound like, and say will vary as you cross from a business meeting to a social gathering, from a formal setting to a casual setting.

When you enter a new culture, at first you may not be physically or verbally adept at mimicking its customary behaviors. You will need to be alert mentally to observe and recognize the behaviors that are customary and effective in different situations. This requires having the observation skills to perceive a specific emotion and its meaning in what others look like or sound like or in what they say. Knowing when and how to kiss, bow, or shake hands takes practice and feedback.

Your motivation and spirit of resilience to try and try again will contribute to your ability to spot the cultural cues in a setting and mimic the customary behaviors with some accuracy. On a recent project in South Africa, the majority of the people with whom I worked spoke Xhosa as their first language, and they graciously spoke English with me. Xhosa is a beautiful language that uses a variety of clicking sounds. As much as I try, I have yet to master even one of these clicks. However, my genuine efforts to learn to mimic the clicks and repeated failure created an atmosphere of humor, acceptance, and friendship.

Building intercultural know-how begins with building your cultural intelligence, the combination of your body, mind, and spirit. Even though our values and behaviors have been hard-wired through our family and society, we can override our automatic, knee-jerk response with awareness, determination, and the ability to get back up after we stumble.

Scan Your Cultural Intelligence

Circle the numbers next to those statements that you believe to be true about yourself or your team. The results of this scan will help guide you in setting your cultural intelligence goals.

1. I know that people of other cultures have different ways of looking at the world, and I have a desire to adopt or understand their perspectives.

2. I do not rely on others to interpret my words and actions to people on my team.

3. I believe that thinking and planning in advance how to adjust what I look like, sound like, and say will not compromise my authenticity.

4. I expect that I will sometimes have to explain or adjust my sense of humor or perspective to those who are not from the same culture as I am.

5. My best efforts to change my speaking style are usually successful, so I do not have to rely on diplomacy and people skills to speak for me.

6. I change my eye contact, greetings, gestures, and other body language to fit in with or mimic people from different cultures.

7. I help to manage the miscommunications that can occur between people who speak plainly and directly and people who speak politely and indirectly.

8. I alter the way I speak to accommodate people who do not share my native language.

9. I am interested in working on global assignments that will require me to work with or influence people of cultures that are different from mine.

10. I am not averse to engaging in activities that may make me self-conscious or have a likelihood of initial failure.

Count your circles to determine your score. If your score is

8–10 You have a solid foundation of cultural intelligence. You are open to ways to engage your mind, body, and spirit of motivation to be culturally intelligent.

5–7 You have some way to go in developing your CQ and in building self-confidence to be effective across cultures. Reexamine the statements you didn't circle and keep them in mind as you read the next section.

0–4 Cultural intelligence is an important area of development for you. Make it a goal to find and apply the actions, tools, and best practices that can help you to develop your CQ.

CULTURAL INTELLIGENCE
Actions, Tools, and Best Practices

Below is a list of actions, tools, and best practices that will help you cultivate your cultural intelligence.

- *Eliminate cultural blind spots.* Becoming aware of how you currently use your attention and how to use your attention better is challenging. In our multitasking, highly distracting work environments, we are bombarded with so much information and by many people who expect an immediate response. The solution is to try to slow the situation down and learn how to catch yourself when you misunderstand something. This means you will need to notice when others who are culturally more adept see that you don't get it. If everyone else knows something but you, you have a blind spot. To eliminate blind spots, stop talking, ask for clarification or feedback, and listen to what you hear.

- *Build your self-efficacy.* Set goals that are within your control to achieve. For example, learn basic social gestures and greetings.

- *Begin to notice the behaviors or speaking habits of others that trigger your negative thinking or stereotypes about people of another culture.* Make it a goal to reframe how you think about these behaviors. Decide to replace your negative thoughts with neutral or positive interpretations.

- *Gain control of your behavior.* Plan to shift your mind-set when you cross cultural boundaries so you can catch yourself when you are on automatic pilot in your thoughts and reactions. This means that you will have to prepare before you cross into another culture and to plan how you want to think. In the heat of the moment in an important business meeting, it will do you little good to have filled your head with facts about the other person's culture and to have rehearsed the appropriate behaviors if you allow yourself to lapse into automatic, habitual behavior.

■ *Take that next global assignment and try to learn the language.* Research has found that the more experience you have working in an international environment and communicating in a foreign language, the greater your ability to flexibly adopt culturally appropriate behavior in general. Feedback from your previous cross-cultural experience—failures and successes—interacting with people of other cultures strengthens your mental ability to recognize the different characteristics or dimensions of culture and helps you more effectively adapt to them. Your mental ability to be aware of and self-correct your perceptions and stereotyping helps you avoid traps of bias and eliminate blind spots. Similarly, experience conducting business in a language that is not your native language broadens your awareness of the challenges of communicating. Familiarity with the many meanings of a phrase, inflection, or pace helps you to be careful in your own word choice, tone, and speed.[5]

Cultural Dimensions

We will now look at the implications of cultural dimensions on your ability to influence results. An assumption throughout this book is that learning influence strategies alone will not serve you in the global business environment. To succeed in influencing across cultures you will need a range of influence strategies, a repertoire or playlist from which to choose, and role models you can emulate. The true test is in the application of the strategies with people of many cultures. And there is no right answer. No one-size-fits-all influence strategy will always be effective because of the multidimensional individuals or groups you will want to influence. The preparation is in the heart, head, and body and in an understanding of the likely dilemmas each cultural encounter may pose.

Extensive study in the multidisciplinary fields of cross-cultural research, applied social psychology, and anthropology recognizes that cultural values manifest themselves in recurring practices, patterns, and behaviors. These are referred to as "dimensions" of culture.

Dimensions are observable and recurring patterns of behavior, practices, and values that can be attributed to regional clusters, for example, the Middle East, Southern Asia, Latin America, Eastern Europe, sub-Saharan Africa, or the Nordic countries. Within any regional cluster, a mix of dimensions of culture may be observed.

Because of the globalization of business, understanding cultural differences is important for people seeking to influence across boundaries. As you work with others across international borders, you are likely to encounter different perceptions of what constitutes appropriate business behavior. Once you learn to recognize the clues of cultural dimensions at work, the practices and values within a specific business or social environment will shed light on what influences an individual's or group's perceptions and interactions. When you make an effort to make these dimensions compatible, interactions can be smooth and productive. When differences are ignored or seen as opposition, misunderstandings can emerge and turn into difficult situations or conflict. Violate unspoken expectations for basic professional introductions, conduct, and dress, for example, and the result can be negative—and lasting—first impressions.

To introduce you to some of the widely accepted dimensions of culture at a very high level, figure 1 offers some examples of cultural dimensions and recognizable behavioral clues to look for when identifying them.[6] For the purpose of illustrating one useful application of this research, five common interpersonal dilemmas are provided. Each will need to be reconciled to get on with the business of delivering results: approach to teamwork, the significance of power and status, the importance of task versus relationship, communication, and orientation to time. For each of these five dilemmas, the related cultural dimensions are described. We will further explore the dimensions of culture as they apply to influence, collaboration, and conflict management in the chapters to come.

I liken the process of addressing a cross-cultural interpersonal dilemma to the experience of my daughter, Emily, as a competitive equestrian. Emily competes as an eventer, which means she competes

COMMON INTERPERSONAL DILEMMA TO RECONCILE **Approach to Teamwork**	
Individualistic ←——— CULTURAL DIMENSION ——→ *Collectivistic*	
Uses "I." Stresses individual accountability, freedom, independence, and mobility. Emphasizes personal objectives and interests. Is a self-starter, takes initiative, and completes tasks without direction. Takes credit. Expresses admiration of individual achievement. Looks after self and immediate family.	Uses "we." Does not call attention to oneself. Emphasizes group interdependence, accountability, loyalty, and commitment. Allows interests of group to prevail. Gives top priority to the good of the whole rather than the individual. Shares resources and credit. Considers direct confrontation rude and undesirable. Believes social network is primary. Encourages and rewards group action and distribution of resources. Expresses pride in and admiration of group achievement.

COMMON INTERPERSONAL DILEMMA TO RECONCILE **Significance of Power and Status**	
Egalitarianism ←——— CULTURAL DIMENSION ——→ *Hierarchy*	
Interacts without overt recognition of power and status. Managers are consultative. Employees prefer being consulted. Employees resist dependence on managers, will contradict them, and will be emotional, friendly, and informal with managers.	Recognizes power, status, and hierarchy. Expects and accepts that power is distributed unequally. Consults with and supports initiatives of superiors. Managers use authoritarian or paternalistic style, providing for employees' needs but without great freedom or responsibilities, which employees prefer. Employees depend on bosses, are afraid of or are unlikely to openly disagree with them or to be emotional or familiar with them.

COMMON INTERPERSONAL DILEMMA TO RECONCILE **Importance of Task versus Relationship**	
Performance and task oriented (low context) ←——— CULTURAL DIMENSION ——→ *Cooperation and relationship oriented (high context)*	
Is direct. Asserts opinion. Appears stern. Believes in importance of transactions, tasks, and facts first. May appear loud and interrupts others. Appears self-assured and may appear arrogant. Appears to act regardless of cues in the setting, i.e., low context or situational awareness. Is competitive. Strives to win. Creates opportunities for personal advancement, higher earnings, and recognition. Accepts conflict and confrontation.	Is indirect. Listens for cues in the setting about how to adapt tone and behavior, i.e., high context. Emphasizes relationship first, transaction later. Desires to please. Strives to have good relationship with direct superior, cooperative relationships with coworkers, and high quality of life. Strives for win-win solution. Resists standing out. Is modest.

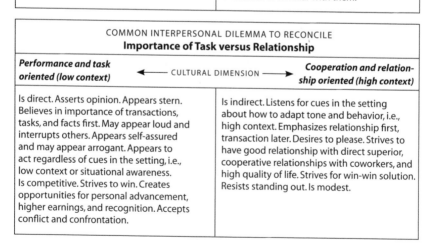

Figure 1 Interpersonal dilemmas and behavioral clues to cultural dimensions

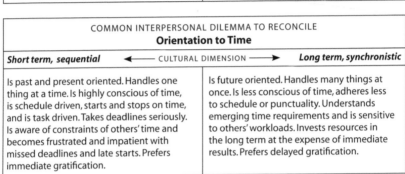

Figure 1 (continued)

at her skill level in dressage, stadium jumping, and cross-country. Cross-country is a test that requires the horse and rider to ride through open fields, woods, and streams over a series of challenging jumps or obstacles within an optimum period of time. Each obstacle is deliberately constructed by the course designer to pose certain questions or dilemmas to the rider. Given this obstacle's height, width, twist, turn, number of in-and-out poles, or room to approach, what strategy is the rider required to use to successfully complete it? In preparation for this event, the rider is allowed to walk the entire course and consider what question or dilemma the course designer is asking the rider to address when she presents her horse to each of the fifteen obstacles. It's a test, and Emily wants to understand the questions. As she walks the course, alone or with her trainer, Emily examines each jump from multiple angles, the approach, the landing, and the footing. She sets her strategy in advance and visualizes herself as she slows down or speeds up the horse, approaches the jump straight on or at an angle, and lengthens or shortens the horse's stride. Competitive riding is a very unforgiving sport that is full of immediate and direct feedback— the horse refuses the jump, the rider zigs (and falls) when the horse zags, rain causes the footing you had yesterday to deteriorate into a muddy pit.

Similarly, you will be presented with questions or dilemmas you will need to address with each individual's and group's dimensions of culture. Knowing the various dimensions and clues to look for will help you identify the questions or dilemmas you will face. This knowledge, along with your head, heart, and body CQ, will help you prepare your approach, footing, and landing before you get started.

Scan Your Need to Learn about Cultural Dimensions

Circle the numbers next to those statements that you believe to be true about yourself or your team. The results of this scan will help guide you in setting your cross-cultural goals regarding cultural dimensions.

1. I know the difference between people from cultures that are more "I" oriented, who frequently emphasize self-interests, and people from cultures that are more "we" oriented, who more frequently emphasize group interests.

2. I am aware that people from some cultural groups accept and defer to my judgment as their manager and other cultural groups prefer to be asked for their opinions.

3. I am aware that members of some cultures generally feel responsible and freer to challenge a statement or assumption I make, whereas members of other cultures accept and defer to my authority as their superior.

4. I observe when people become frustrated with peers or team members who display a more polite, indirect, and nonconfrontational style even when they are encouraged to speak up for themselves.

5. I am careful to avoid publicly blaming or praising individual performance in culturally mixed groups; some individuals would feel this action may jeopardize personal "face."

6. I am aware of the tension that can arise in multicultural work groups when some members attempt to precisely articulate a course of action or decision and others are more willing to manage within more ambiguous guidelines.

7. I notice the difference between those who promote a course of action that will pay off in the long run and those who advocate an immediate return on investment.

8. I manage meetings and projects where some individuals are rigid in their expectations to start and stop on time and adhere to a precise agenda and deliverables; other members are less likely to hold to precise deadlines, consider themselves more fluid in their adjustment to schedules, and flexibly reinterpret outcomes.

9. I am careful to observe when some members may be offended by what they consider to be another's immodest self-promotion and emphasis of personal achievements.

10. I am willing to take the time to speak privately to individual members of the team or decision-making group as a starting point for discussion and decision making.

Count your circles to determine your score. If your score is

8–10 You apply your understanding of dimensions of culture in your everyday work life. Make it your goal to tell your team about the differences you observe and accept and how you choose to blend them.

5–7 You have a basic or growing familiarity with some dimensions of culture and are applying what you know. Continue to sharpen your observation skills and to optimize the differences within your team.

0–4 Dimensions of culture is an important area of development for you. Many actions, tools, and best practices are available to help you develop your observation skills. Begin by selecting from among the activities suggested in this chapter and identifying a role model.

The International Business Culture

Researchers ask if globalization will cause a convergence of international business cultures and if individual dimensions of culture will eventually disappear. So far, there is no evidence of a convergence toward one international business culture or global management style in multinational organizations. No single leadership influence style prevails as a one-size-fits-all solution.[7]

However, interesting research has identified situations or conditions where the international business culture's values, norms, and beliefs may supersede or override an individual's own culture.[8] That is, an individual is less likely to behave independently of the behavioral norms of the business culture if that business culture is "strong." A strong business culture has clear behavioral norms, unambiguous expectations and values, and a shared set of beliefs about how to succeed and fail.[9] A "weak" business culture has unclear or mixed signals about behavior, contradictory messages about values, and ambiguity about the norms that might dictate or guide perceptions and beliefs. The stronger the business culture, the more likely individuals will interact more uniformly and the less likely their native cultures will influence their behavior.

Another finding of this research in strong business cultures is that stress causes people to revert to their personal dimensions' automatic response system, which overrides the influences of the organization. For example, you may put aside the idiosyncratic behaviors and values of your personal culture to perform business in your international organization. But when you and your teammates are pressured to perform under aggressive time constraints, your individual cultural hard-wiring will take over. The greater the pressure, the more likely your cognitive reasoning will shut down in favor of your most well-rehearsed, impulsive, and automatic responses of your native culture. The more experience you have performing under pressure, the greater the amount of pressure you will be able to tolerate before this happens.

Be prepared for individual cultural practices, including your own, to emerge and amplify under pressure. Learning to recognize dimensions of culture when you and your team are not in crisis mode will help you influence cohesion and alignment when the going gets rough.

For example, different cultures have different concepts of teamwork and how to get results. Some cultures favor independence and individualism, while other cultures favor interdependence and collective action. A team may quickly run into difficulties when colleagues from an individualistic culture who value self-starters and take individual initiative to complete tasks are working side by side with colleagues from a more collectivistic culture. Their collectivistic counterparts value group-focused behavior, expect to get direction from their superiors, and do not want to call attention to themselves.

Status can pose its own predicaments because some cultures are more egalitarian, while others are more hierarchical. People from egalitarian cultures give little recognition to someone's formal position power and status. They may address their superiors by their first or given names, be openly friendly and informal with them, disagree and debate an issue publicly, and feel a responsibility to surface tough questions. People from hierarchical cultures, on the other hand, pay more attention to a person's power and status in the organization. They will publicly defer to the authority of another and concede to a superior's wishes or opinions. These different cultural values about professional behavior can lead to tension if they are not understood and appreciated.

How consensus might be reached is another example of cultural dimensions in action. Decision making is a critical management activity and is another subset of culture. In a Japanese corporation, for example, which is more collectivist than individualist, decision making is based on extensive behind-the-scenes discussions with all interested parities, a practice called *nemawashi*. A decision is made after soliciting input from and securing the commitment of everyone affected by the decision. In this culture, which is long-term oriented, this process requires time for the decision makers to learn each stakeholder's feelings and opinions firsthand. It may include speaking to the direct reports of other managers or line employees who touch the process or who have a stake in the outcome of the decision. This investment of time in the short term is expected to yield better results in terms of greater team cohesion and commitment to the decision by those who must execute it.

In a Japanese corporation, the executive committee would not be a decision-making forum as it is in Western corporations. In the Japanese example, when an issue comes before the executive committee, the decision has already been made through the *nemawashi* process. Each member of the committee has already been approached, discussed the decision, and agreed to it. The executive committee members announce the agreement among themselves and lay plans of execution. The responsibility for the decision is shared. Meetings may be shorter because deliberation has taken place outside of them. No last-minute personal objections are raised that might reopen a discussion. Line employees have been brought along in the decision-making process from the beginning. They understand the issue because they have been consulted, and they are able to see the rationale for the decision they will have to execute. The group is primary; relations with others are more important than anyone's personal opinion or self-interest.

Decisions will be made very differently when a more Western or individualistic and direct management style is employed. Here the expectation is that debate will be held openly in meetings. Managers leading the issue may come to the meeting having already "campaigned," but this may be viewed more as political wrangling and bartering than consensus seeking. Meetings are expected to be forums for open and even heated debate. The most senior leader may eventually rise as the final arbiter, summarize the various positions aired, state the decision, and assign various next steps to those in the room.

Individual commitment to this decision remains, however, problematic. In the more individualistic Western culture, the decision is open to further debate. Executive committee members report back to their dotted-line managers in other parts of the organization. The reactions to executive committee decisions are funneled back to the senior leader in a private meeting—often in an effort to sway the senior leader's opinion and change the decision. This decision-making process is in stark contrast to the more collectivist Eastern management style, where no one would publicly confront someone else or cause someone to lose face in public.

The fundamental difference in management styles is very clear. Now imagine how Eastern and Western regional companies that were once virtually autonomous begin to share resources and make decisions to do business together in a matrix organization.

How might leaders of multinational companies anticipate and prevent problems caused by different cultural and social assumptions about what constitutes effective management behaviors? And how do they structure in those behaviors? They need to support them with formal organizational systems and policies. What can an organization's leadership do to create a culture that encourages and reinforces the desired management and employee behaviors? What are the culturally appropriate behaviors in a multicultural workplace? That depends, as you'll see in this story.

CASE STUDY
Chad Williams and Cultural Dimensions

Chad Williams has spent twenty years doing business around the world and was the man in the middle as cross-cultural differences played out.

"I was working with a team of native-Portuguese-speaking businesspeople in Brazil and our native-Chinese-speaking team counterparts in Hong Kong. I had been in Brazil and Hong Kong for some time on different assignments. The Brazilians liked me and often let me in on their jokes about us British. They frequently humored me by acknowledging whenever I had written a report or lengthy e-mail. They repeated a common colloquialism they used: 'The British like to write, so let the British write, but we have no intention of reading what they wrote.' Theirs is an oral culture.

"However, their Chinese counterparts were recognized for remaining politely quiet on conference calls. They would follow up the calls with lengthy written communiqués that were essentially being ignored by the Brazilians. The team was at an impasse: the Brazilians' attempts to orally draw out the Chinese were ignored; the Chinese reports went unread."

This dilemma in communication preferences was bridged only by a common language, English, spoken within team meetings, but informally, regional cultural practices and values trumped the formal corporate culture. Both the Brazilian and Chinese cultures were fundamentally relationship oriented, and neither the Brazilians nor the Chinese wanted to jeopardize the relationship, cause others to lose face, or presume to inflict their preferences on others.

Chad wanted to get the two groups together to tackle this dilemma and create an approach that might reconcile the differences, but international travel was prohibited due to budget constraints.

"I thought the quickest approach would be to just serve as diplomatic liaison between the two worlds. I was confident we all shared a common interest in delivering the same result. This was a big help. But as much as I tried to get the groups to meet each other halfway in their back-and-forth communication, it never worked. As soon as I was out of the middle, both sides fell back to their ways.

"Here's the thing," Chad said. "The time it took to have every conversation twice, to write back and forth twice as many times, put at least an extra three months onto the project. And the costs of these high-level experts on both sides were not cheap. Corporate-wide recognition of this issue and training to build skills to overcome it would have helped. We just don't have the time to send everyone around the world to learn about these cultural differences firsthand."

So what's the solution? How might Chad have tackled this another way? Would it help if the team had a common understanding of the predictable communication dilemmas they were likely to encounter and a shared vocabulary and forum to work them out? Could Chad respectfully describe or facilitate a discussion—with written and visual references—including his observations of these dimensions playing themselves out?

Chad decided it was worth a try and took three small but meaningful steps. First, Chad presented a list of the many times the Chinese and Brazilian team members were actually in agreement but missed each others' meanings. They mistook their communication failures for disagreement. This got everyone's attention. Second, he asked the group if they might be able to compromise by working to improve both their written e-mails and their oral skills. They agreed to each submit samples of their e-mails to an international business writing coach for private feedback and to participate in a two-hour virtual refresher geared to their needs. Finally, Chad introduced the team to Dr. Culture, whom you will meet shortly.

CULTURAL DIMENSIONS
Actions, Tools, and Best Practices

Gaining familiarity with the various dimensions of culture and the dilemmas or questions you will face is a very important step in building your cross-cultural know-how. Set achievable goals to develop this resource and select from among the actions, tools, and best practices below to fill in your action plan.

- *Begin by understanding the basics about dimensions of culture (see the references at the end of the book) and identify which dimensions best describe you.* Then try to identify the dimensions of culture of your peers, team members, managers, stakeholders, and anyone else on whom you depend to get your job done and need to influence. For example, if you know you will be working on a team of electronic engineers from India, Germany, and Japan and you are a marketing analyst and native-born Eastern European, you can expect to encounter a number of cultures, including the subcultures of the different functions.

- *Target one culture at a time.* Compare and contrast your own culture (values, behaviors, beliefs, rituals) to another culture. For example, what have you noticed about the way you give your opinion and feedback and how others on your team react to you? How do you demonstrate frustration? How does this compare to others on your team? How do you regard a deadline? How is this similar to or different from how others think?

- *Introduce your team to your and their dimensions of culture and those of your target cultures.* Investigate further the significant research regarding the values, attitudes, behaviors, and beliefs of different cultures. Learn about those aspects of your native culture relative to the other cultures you will encounter, depend upon to deliver your results, and ultimately want to influence. You can find a number of interactive, web-based tools on the market to identify your dimensions of culture, the dimensions of each of your team members, and those of other key stakeholders (see the references).

You now have a sense of the mental, emotional, and physical elements of the cultural intelligence you will want to cultivate and have been introduced to the dimensions of culture that you are likely to encounter in a variety of predictable business settings. It is now time to apply these insights to your ability to be understood throughout your cross-cultural business communications. And to meet Dr. Culture.

Cross-Cultural Communication

Communicating effectively across diverse cultures means conveying information in a way that includes and can be understood by people of other cultures and native languages in a manner that recognizes, affirms, and values the worth of individuals. This is a very pragmatic application of your cognitive, motivational, and physical cultural intelligence. Failure to build self-awareness and the ability to self-correct to improve your cross-cultural communication skills will come at a price. People you depend on around the world may not understand you. And frustrated with the effort it takes to communicate, they may give up and fall silent, blocking access to critical information, resources, and the cooperation you need to deliver results.

Scan Your Cross-Cultural Communication Practices

Circle the numbers next to those statements that you believe to be true about yourself or your team. The results of this scan will point you to areas you will want to focus on.

1. I am managing a team initiative in a region or regions where I do not reside.

2. I have scheduled a meeting with international participants where one or more native English speakers dominated the conversation.

3. I am aware of the degree to which others are able to understand me when I speak.

4. Some people in my meetings or on my international business calls are nonnative English speakers.

5. Some members of my team speak English with a regional accent that is difficult for some to understand.

6. I have grown frustrated with silent members in my meetings that I need and expect to share information, expertise, or perspective.

7. Some members of my team or stakeholders use business jargon, technical terminology, or regional colloquialisms that not everyone understands.

8. Some members of my team are under pressure that may cause stress sufficient to distract or diminish their ability to listen and understand.

9. Some members of my team may occasionally feel left out of conversations that take place in a language that is not their native language.

10. The majority of my team and stakeholder meetings are conducted on the phone.

Count your circles to determine your score. If your score is

7–10 Your team is culturally diverse and communicating under stressful conditions. You and your team need Dr. Culture's Culture-o-Meter and cross-culture communication coaching.

4–6 You and your team need cross-cultural communication support. Plan to improve the chances of having clear and open lines of communication by targeting some of the solutions Dr. Culture suggests.

0–3 Communicating across cultures may not be an immediate need for your team. Read Dr. Culture's advice and see how close your "best practices" align with his.

Being understood and understanding others is the basis of communication. If you and your team cannot understand each other due to language proficiency, rich accents, or bad habits, you need help now. To introduce ways to be understood by other cultures, let's meet an important subject-matter expert, Dr. Culture.

CASE STUDY
Dr. Culture

The situation is critical. A corporate team is gathered around a speakerphone on an important conference call that pulls together partners from across the globe. Words are coming from the phone. The language is English, but the words make no sense. One brave participant asks for clarification on a key point, but the speaker rushes to the next topic. Another participant asks a pointed question in hopes of understanding. The reply is a nonsensical jumble of jargon. Everyone's speaking the same language, but no one is communicating. The project is in peril. It's time to call in Dr. Culture—*stat.*

We've all been in an international conversation where we have felt ineffective, misunderstood, or in this case, ignored. English may well be the international language of business, but speaking the same language does not mean we will comprehend each other. That's because communication is more than language. It's culture: the collective values, norms, and beliefs that influence how we act, think, and speak. Native speakers of a language are usually unaware of how their own habits of speech and cultural norms contribute to communication breakdown with nonnative speakers.

When communication breaks down, Dr. Culture is the man for the job.

Dr. Culture's Culture-o-Meter

Dr. Culture is a bit of a mad scientist. He has invented the Culture-o-Meter, which records and analyzes intercultural speech patterns and behaviors while simultaneously improving them. Not only does his patented Culture-o-Meter provide a standard printout of your personal results, but an automatic reward-and-penalty response unit prompts more effective behavior. Communicate effectively and you receive an Appreciation and Approval reward—an instantaneous and pleasant happiness sensation in your brain. Fail to meet Dr. Culture's standards and you'll receive a Displeasure and Disapproval penalty, which is a mild clench in the stomach, similar to the feeling you get when you realize you've misspoken or acted inappropriately in front of your grandmother.

The Culture-o-Meter is widely used by the most successful global business leaders. The improvements in cross-cultural communication and influence skills it has delivered have dramatically improved business results while boosting team performance and personal engagement and satisfaction scores.

Here's how it works: Before meeting a new colleague, joining a conference call, or attending a meeting, individuals undergo a series of diagnostic tests to help calibrate their speech and cross-cultural effectiveness. The gauges on the Culture-o-Meter are displayed like an automobile dashboard in full view of Dr. Culture and the subject of the evaluation.

The Culture-o-Meter dashboard has five gauges: the Jargon-o-Meter, the Speedometer, the Context-o-Meter, the Diction-o-Meter, and the Adapt-o-Meter.

Jargon-o-Meter. Like a battery charge gauge on an automobile, the range on the Jargon-o-Meter runs from "weak" to "strong." The "weak" end indicates use of language that excludes, strains, and eventually drains the ability of others to comprehend and follow the conversation. You will see a yellow warning light when you use colloquialisms, acronyms, business jargon, or technical terminology that only a member of the tightest in-group or a subject-matter expert would recognize and understand. When you see the yellow warning light, you are given time to immediately rephrase—make a simultaneous translation—using terms the listener can understand. Overuse of jargon or failure to adjust your language will make your gauge light turn red.

In the extreme, the use of exclusive, in-group language is the verbal equivalent of a secret handshake. This is rarely deliberate. Usually it's an unconscious habit of speech among familiars. Nonetheless, its continued use will result in a Displeasure and Disapproval clench to your stomach.

The "strong" end of the Jargon-o-Meter spectrum indicates the use of inclusive language, which means that the speaker is able to address the greatest number of listeners of any native language and be understood. Success is rewarded with an instantaneous sensation of Appreciation and Approval.

Speedometer. Similar to the speedometer on an automobile, the Culture-o-Meter's Speedometer gauge measures the speaker's rate of speech and transitions from one topic to another. The range is from "too slow" to "too fast." The gauge has a unique "ideal" center. This ideal, like a speed limit, varies based on the terrain or context of the conversation—in this case, the dominant language and diversity of cultures in the conversation. Dr. Culture's research shows some business or regional cultures have a very brisk and crisp pace of speaking, thinking aloud, publicly debating issues, and coming to conclusions. Rapid speech in these cultures may signal competence, intelligence, or authority. However, in other business and regional cultures, it is customary to employ a slower, more deliberate pace that allows time for pauses, internal private thoughts, and reflection. Discussing or debating a topic publicly may not be appropriate in such cultures.

Speak or move too slowly and you risk allowing the listener's mind to wander. You may also appear to be patronizing your listener or to be uninformed. Speak or move too fast and your audience may be unable to keep up to absorb and mentally process what you are saying. Both extremes will give you the Displeasure and Disapproval penalty. The optimum score is achieved when you find the ideal rate of speech for each audience that results in increased comprehension and engagement. You are rewarded with Appreciation and Approval.

When the gauge's yellow warning light flashes, you can adjust your rate of speech and movement through the agenda by simply becoming aware of your rate and how it compares to others'. Listen carefully to and try to emulate the speech rate of someone you know to be effective in being heard and understood. If, as you speak, you imagine sentence punctuation—the periods, commas, and question marks—and deliberately pause at each, you will slow your rate of speech considerably.

Context-o-Meter. The Context-o-Meter is very sophisticated and a unique invention of Dr. Culture. It is calibrated to analyze situational variables that will influence the speaker's effectiveness. Specifically, Dr. Culture wants speakers to know if their delivery strategy is appropriate based on situational cues such as the self-interests or group interests of the audience, organizational direction, political climate, discussion objectives, and, yes, culture.

The Context-o-Meter ranges between "too indirect" and "too direct" and is calibrated to both the corporate and regional culture or cultures in a meeting. Dr. Culture knows that high-context cultures are those that value relational sensitivity. In other words, a strong foundation of respect and social sensitivity must be laid before substantive discussion can take place. In these cultures, direct corrective feedback to an individual in the presence of others would be totally inappropriate. The difficulty comes when speakers are too direct. If they disregard the relationships, status, image, or reputation of their audience, they may fail to win the minds of the listeners.

In a low-context setting or culture, directness, candor, and a forthright "cut-to-the-chase" approach may be valued. The transaction is of greatest importance, not how it is conducted. If speakers are too indirect, they may become imprecise or ramble and fail to get to the heart of the matter. This may be due to extreme sensitivity to the relationship, political climate, or fear of punishment or failure. Whatever the rationale, the audience is lost and confused.

A yellow warning light on the Context-o-Meter lets speakers know if they need to become more direct or to pull back and be more sensitive to the positions and relationships of others. In the end, speakers need to balance getting to the heart of the matter while still being aware of the parameters or boundaries that can exist in any context.

Diction-o-Meter. Dr. Culture designed the Diction-o-Meter to resemble the fuel level indicator on an automobile. It registers word articulation and tone modulation. The range is from "empty" to "full." "Full" indicates the ideal, with speakers using their own true, rich regional accent while still being totally comprehensible and expressive enough to engage the listener. "Empty," on the other hand, indicates a flat, monotone, inarticulate, or robotic delivery. Such delivery fails to interest the listener or to clarify the importance of the message. Thankfully, Dr. Culture has included another yellow caution light that reminds the speaker to check in with the listeners to ensure they comprehend.

Take the example of one of my favorite managers, Bob, who has a beautifully rich Irish brogue. He also habitually speaks at a very brisk pace and with caustic wit and biting humor. The faster he speaks, the more pronounced his accent and garbled his words, and he can become completely incomprehensible to anyone unfamiliar with the cadence and pronunciations of his accent. If Bob becomes impatient, his tone grows strong and fierce, and he's even harder to understand. His listeners feel his urgency to do something but do not always know what to do or why. The result is confusion, a sense of exclusion, a withholding of information, resistance, and a loss of momentum.

The costs of confusion and failure to share information were high enough for Bob to engage Dr. Culture and use his Culture-o-Meter to adjust his style. As a result of this analysis, Bob now deliberately thinks about his diction on international calls. He now says each sound in every word. At first, this hyper-self-conscious diction was extremely awkward for Bob, and his compatriots teased him. But his multilingual team recognized and appreciated his efforts and rewarded him with better input and action.

Adapt-o-Meter. The Adapt-o-Meter indicates the climate of the conversation and, like a tachometer on an automobile, helps a speaker know when to adapt and shift gears. Using a scale of one to six, the gauge measures conversational revolutions per minute. The higher the number, the faster you are moving through material and concepts and the greater the strain on your audience. But if the revolutions drop too low, your conversation will sputter and stall out. Both of these situations will result in a Displeasure and Disapproval gut clench from the Culture-o-Meter. Finding and creating the optimum climate of pressure is critical to the cross-cultural influencer. It is the motor that runs the vehicle.

Like the driver of a standard-shift automobile, a speaker must watch this gauge carefully and listen for any sounds of strain in the audience to know when to shift up or down. The speaker must pause and check in regularly to confirm the audience accurately understands the intended message and urgency.

The Benefits of a Culture-o-Meter

If Dr. Culture and his machine really did exist and could help calibrate every participant in a meeting or conference call so that everyone spoke in a comprehensible and inclusive manner, what difference might this make?

One senior executive told his regional leadership that if they could all improve the quality of their communication with their business partners and peers around the world by just 5 percent , the savings in time wasted in frustration, misunderstanding, withheld information, and disrupted relationships would be exponential. What do you estimate the difference would be in your organization?

Saving Face Before You Lose It

Using the Culture-o-Meter will also decrease the time and effort spent managing "face"—that is, ensuring no one is humiliated or disrespected in a public forum. Managing face is directly related to communication habits and cultural climates. Imagine that each participant in a meeting has critical information and needs to feel included and safe in order to share it. If any participants feel intimidated or fear ridicule or shame, they may feel devalued and may withhold their important information. If, however, they feel included and important, their fear of losing face declines and they may be more willing to open up and fully share their resources.[10]

The many small but effective adjustments that can be made by using Dr. Culture's Culture-o-Meter result in better communication—and ultimately influence—across cultural boundaries. The walk toward cultural intelligence—rethinking how we think, building self-awareness and sufficient motivation to risk making initial mistakes, and speaking in an inclusive and comprehensible manner—is paved with payoffs. Once you have your head and heart ready and your body hooked up to Dr. Culture's fantasy dashboard, you're on your way to enjoying the rewards of speaking cross-culturally.

Dominant Culture Blind Side

Dr. Culture highlights how native-language speakers of the "most preferred" language of any group are prone to violate the "rules" of being understood. This is a predictable dynamic of the dominant culture in any group. Members of the dominant group are less likely to notice this dynamic than people in subordinate groups.

Because English is the language of international business and finance, native and near-native English speakers will be at a distinct advantage in a cross-cultural conversation. They are more likely to assume the "most preferred" dominant status, and speakers of other languages the "least preferred" subordinate status. Beware of this potential blind side, especially when you are not in a formal business setting.

Here's how one seasoned and sophisticated native-English-speaking international manager confirmed this dynamic. A native English speaker, he had problems with the dominant culture blind side.

"Until just recently I used to let my guard down every time we broke for coffee or drinks after a long day. As soon as I moved into informal off-line gatherings, I'd lapse back into my familiar slang and fast pace. Before I knew it, I'd be surrounded by others I've known for years and who look like and talk just like me. I realized in hindsight I literally lost years of networking and building relationships that I paid for later. I missed out on information shared in informal conversations and some of the give-and-take exchanges of small favors."

Native-language speakers who are in the dominant culture of informal conversations need to include all nonnative speakers equally. Wait till you get off the plane at home to indulge in familiar colloquialisms or save them for one-on-one phone calls when you are sure the other person will understand you.

Communication and Stress

Another potential blind side is stress. People can absorb very little of what you are saying when they are anxious. During times of extraordinary stress, people's ability to hear is diminished. You may be informing your team about changes and setting out proof about how the changes are relevant to their self-interests. Your audience may *hear* you talking, but they will have difficulty *understanding* what the message means to them personally if they already fear what the message will mean. Their fear and anxiety may be the result of the accumulated stress of change after change. This makes Dr. Culture's advice especially important when people in your audience are not native or near-native English speakers.

People will need to hear a clear, concise message (your minimal and memorable message from chapter 1) over and over and over again in order to be sold on a rational level and move into committed action (see "The Central Route to Influence" in chapter 3). You, as the leader, may lose your motivation or heart with all this repetition. Please remember, the higher your position in the hierarchy, the sooner you are privy to information, so you have had more time to adjust to the information and meaning of a change. You will become frustrated with this repetition of the same information far sooner than your audience will be from hearing it.

Your own stress may build as you feel your audience is just not getting it. Your impatience will show up physically and may undermine your original intention to adjust your behavior to the cultural mix of your audience. Your tone of voice, your expressions, and your posture may appear more direct and authoritative just when the group requires openness for questions, patience, listening, and understanding. Some cultures dictate that it is rude to publicly question authority, so questions for clarification may go unasked and unanswered. This is another cultural boundary to cross in order to influence—and another reason to follow Dr. Culture's advice.

Failure to adjust what you sound like and what you say will lead to confusion and exclusion. The case below clearly illustrates the costs of failure to use cross-cultural know-how to influence the attitudes and behaviors of others toward your goal.

CASE STUDY
Robert Lewis and Cross-Cultural Communication

Robert Lewis was managing director of a team of software developers in Colombo, Sri Lanka, from corporate headquarters in Rochester, England. He had never been there and knew next to nothing about the culture or current events of Sri Lanka. He did know, however, that he and his colleagues in Rochester once did the very job these offshore workers were doing. Now Robert and his Rochester-based peers were managing these Sri Lankan workers remotely rather than doing the work themselves or directing people within arm's length. Robert was extremely frustrated with the performance of these Sri Lankan workers.

One of his Rochester-based teammates and comanagers, Pari Kumar, told Robert that he was much feared and consistently made people cry. "They dread their calls with you and your e-mails because they know you are angry and dissatisfied," Pari said.

"I've had it with them," Robert replied. "They can't do the most simple job. Okay, so I yell occasionally and they apologize all over themselves. I do not want them to apologize; I want them to do the job right the first time. I don't want to tell them how to do it. That's why we hired them. They have to be able to figure out how to get the job done there in Sri Lanka, on the ground. If they can't do the job, why don't we just bring the work back here to Rochester, where I don't have to get up in the middle of the night to tell someone how to do it?"

Another manager in the room, Keena Khan, had just finished reading *Anil's Ghost* by Michael Ondaatje, which takes place in Sri Lanka during the civil wars there. Keena said she read of the atrocities and loss of life and political upheaval, the inability to trust authority, and the financial insecurity and tenuous nature of daily living. The civil war was reportedly leveling off in Sri Lanka at that time. Keena said she imagined the lives of the people in Colombo, Sri Lanka, were very different from that of Robert, sitting back here in Rochester.

Robert laughed at Keena for pretending to be an expert on Sri Lanka after reading fiction. She said at least she knew enough to know that people in that part of the world respected authority, relationships were important in work, and people behaved as a group. Keena said she could imagine the sense of relief of the most privileged and educated Sri Lankans coming into the safety of their company's building and the reassurance of receiving a steady paycheck. Robert should know the feeling, she said, because he grew up in the depressed economy of Rochester. He had more in common with his Sri Lankan counterparts than he was willing to admit.

"Take a deep breath before you get on the phone next time. Quit being such a bully," Keena advised.

"Yeah, and slow down. Show a little respect. Lighten up. Whatever you are doing is not working. So try another approach," Pari said.

Robert listened with one ear to his colleagues. His budget did not include travel to Sri Lanka, and he never intended to go there and build relationships with these people. Someone way above his pay grade had promised that his team in Sri Lanka could achieve results for a fraction of the costs. Robert's job was to deliver someone else's promise. He had no experience coaching this level of incompetence up to the pre-outsourcing levels of his former Rochester team. So his Sri Lankan counterparts were not the only ones operating under pressure. Keena was right in one respect: his job was a precious commodity in Rochester, and he had a family to support.

When I met with Robert and his team sometime later, I learned that they were meeting their goals. So what did Robert do?

He acknowledged and reflected on some of the truth in Pari and Keena's assessment. After all, they knew only what he told them, so he assumed he had conveyed the very dynamic he was too blind to see for himself. Stress had diminished both Robert's and his Sri Lankan team's ability to communicate. Robert was oozing anger and frustration, which translated into his tone. He was operating in a direct, task-oriented, and aggressive manner with a culture that was politely indirect, was relationship oriented, and valued sensitivity. He was asking people to show initiative and complete tasks without direction when his Sri Lankan counterparts believed teamwork meant supporting the initiatives and dictates of their superiors. Though Robert was used to a more egalitarian give-and-take relationship with his managers, his team in Sri Lanka was showing Robert the deference and respect they were accustomed to showing people of status and power.

Robert also accepted Pari's and Keena's offers to help him prepare for his next call and he followed their advice. For his next call, Robert decided to start his steppingstone influence strategy from square one.

He clarified the mission, goals, roles, and procedures of his team. He emphasized the need for the team to work together to identify any challenges or roadblocks to getting the job done. In an effort to build relationships, Robert decided to invest time in setting up a schedule to speak with each of the members of his team one-on-one. He always had an agenda and focus question, but he began each call by inquiring after his team member's family. He typed this personal information into his computer's contact list and he shared information about his own family. He used this one-on-one time to give feedback and coaching privately to avoid publicly humiliating anyone on his team.

Robert set up a schedule of rotating team leaders charged with going to each member of the team privately to ensure individual and team performance expectations were clear. He dramatically shifted what he sounded like and what he said.

In addition, he accepted the reality of his shared ownership of his offshore team's results. "I" was not eliminated from Robert's vocabulary—he always spoke for himself when expressing his opinion—but "we" became much more prevalent as he accepted collective responsibility. As Pari and Keena predicted, the team's results improved as the tension diminished and mutual understanding increased.

As you can see by using Dr. Culture's Culture-o-Meter and adjusting your approach, as Robert Lewis did, you can improve your cross-cultural communication skills and improve your results. Applying your cultural intelligence—mind, body, and spirit—you want to think and plan before your next meeting or conference call to consider the communication needs of others. By setting achievable goals, you can bolster your self-confidence and belief in the value of small adjustments.

CROSS-CULTURAL COMMUNICATION
Actions, Tools, and Best Practices

Here is a list of actions, tools, and best practices we can all borrow from Robert and Dr. Culture.

■ *Scan yourself.* Use Dr. Culture's Culture-o-Meter gauges to do an honest assessment of your cross-cultural communication habits. If you are part of the dominant group whose native language is the language spoken with the nonnative speakers present, set a goal to deliberately speak in a way that can be understood. Check in privately with the nonnative-language speakers about the degree to which they are understanding and feel included in the conversation. Remember, the dominants are the last to know.

■ *Introduce your team to Dr. Culture and his Culture-o-Meter.* Decide to have a bit of fun with it. Tell the team how you think you measured on each of the five gauges. Invite team members to privately assess themselves and to give each other feedback on one gauge. Make cross-cultural communication skills an area of feedback in your next one-on-one with each team member.

■ *Scan your audience.* Your ability to influence others will be only as good as your ability to communicate with and your knowledge of each particular audience. Your ability to tailor effective influence strategies to your audience will depend on having some very precise measurements. You'll need binoculars for close observation and finely tuned listening devices.

Begin with the most direct assessment of your audience's proficiency in the language in which the communication will take place. The medium in which the communication will take place will dictate just how important the audience's proficiency is. In a more formal written report, your audience has time to read and reread for total comprehension. They control the pace and the order in which they read and their own critical thinking path. E-mail is a different matter because it has evolved with an expectation of an immediate response. Our e-mail writing and reading are hurried, reduced to acronyms and business jargon, and full of the emotion and tone of the moment. This is a disastrous mix for cross-cultural communication. Face-to-face meetings are a rarity and luxury in international business, but they, as well as video calls, provide some nonverbal cues that affect comprehension.

Scanning your audience requires thoughtful preparation before you begin to communicate to influence. Here are some questions to ask.

- *English proficiency:* What language does your audience speak? Are all of the people on the call or in the meeting native, near-native, or advanced English speakers? If not, how do you propose to adjust your rate of speech and your use of colloquialisms? How do you intend to check in or pause along the way to confirm understanding?
- *Business jargon:* What business- or industry-specific language is your audience accustomed to speaking and hearing? What technical terminology will they find acceptable or overly technical?
- *"Hot buttons":* What words should you avoid because they might provoke a strong negative reaction? For example, if the business has moved away from one strategy because it was the source of failure and is now passé, reference to it may raise feelings of anger or shame. And reference to investment when expenses are being cut could create an immediate negative reaction.

- *Find a role model.* Identify a person you consider to be comprehensible. Consider this person a role model and observe when he catches himself using jargon, slang, or difficult words and how he immediately rephrases.

- *Be more self-conscious.* Commit to six weeks of hyperawareness of how you and others in your dominant language group exercise your Dr. Culture skills. The various gauges in Dr. Culture's Culture-o-Meter reflect the ability not only to be comprehensible but to listen and observe as well. Communication is considered two-way when we balance telling with listening. Asking and listening promotes understanding and eliminates blind spots.

- *Stop talking and listen.* Assess how much is being understood by you and your audience. If you get nothing but silence, try asking a question. Pause to give people time to reflect. If necessary, count silently to yourself to be sure it's a legitimate pause— "one thousand one, one thousand two, one thousand three, one thousand four, one thousand five"—before asking the question in another way. If you do get something back, show you've heard by summarizing the comment.

- *Use privacy.* When giving direct and personal feedback, schedule a one-on-one call to minimize confusion and reduce the risk of someone feeling humiliated or losing face in front of others. When you are in a high-context, highly relational, or group-oriented culture, you can still be your direct self, but you'll be more effective when you do so privately. Choosing the right setting or context in which your communication takes place will avoid public confrontation.

- *Practice "simultaneous translation."* When you hear yourself use a colloquialism, business jargon, or big words, immediately rephrase the concept in terms more universally understood.

- *Speak for yourself.* Make "I" statements when expressing a personal opinion, but wait your turn or ask for forgiveness when and if you feel you must interrupt. In an indirect or collectivistic culture, ask for others' opinions indirectly: "What might be some other ways of considering this?"

- *Before your next business phone call, take one minute—only sixty seconds—to think about your own dimensions of culture.* How might your cultural hard-wiring show up in your communication habits? Select one gauge from Dr. Culture's Culture-o-Meter to monitor yourself. During the call, be aware of how well you understand what is being said by others. Observe how well others on the call understand as well. This process of testing yourself while you are in the midst of learning exercises your brain for better cultural intelligence.

- *Do a post-mortem.* At the end of your next business phone call, analyze and evaluate your own effectiveness at catching on to what was happening on the call. Reevaluate your goals, plans, and assumptions about how best to get the job of a conference call done cross-culturally. Try to do this for one conference call every week.

CROSS-CULTURAL KNOW-HOW
Actions, Tools, and Best Practices

Cross-cultural know-how is a fundamental resource for conducting business internationally and essential to influence across boundaries. We do not have to be multilingual; we have to be culturally intelligent. Our cultural intelligence begins with a desire to be effective with people we encounter. Our mind will be fully engaged as we anticipate, plan for, and strategize about the best approach for every encounter. We will think on-the-fly as we catch stereotypes that distort our thinking and perception of others and create a personal blind side.

Here are a few final tips for building your cross-cultural know-how:

- *Remember that adjusting to accommodate and adapt to other cultures is not about losing your authentic self.* It's about expanding your repertoire or playlist and preparing yourself to be more effective interpersonally and to influence with greater assurance of success.

- *Build your sense of self-efficacy by setting achievable goals.* Remind yourself, using your computer's calendar function, to take an honest look in the mirror about your progress in building and applying your cultural intelligence.

- *Set aside stereotypes.* You may have a history or an experience with people or a single person of another culture that led to your current distrust or dislike. However, as a very successful Nigerian businesswoman told me, "There's no place for discrimination or stereotyping in international business. It's just not practical." Your faith or spiritual beliefs may serve as your reminder for compassion. I agree our stereotypes, fears, and distrust are stitched into each of us at a very early age. They may come from some original basis of painful truth, but they are lies that limit your effectiveness and true spirit of purpose.

- *For the next six weeks, commit to turning off your automatic pilot response mechanism.* Start by noticing the language you use as you dash off e-mails. Be mindful of your reader's ability to understand as well as your desire to be understood.

At this point we have discussed the importance of strategically positioning your idea or initiative within your organization and ways to do this. You are now mentally alert to the need to develop your cultural intelligence, aware of predictable dilemmas you will encounter with different dimensions of culture, and equipped with a set of gauges to monitor and improve your comprehensibility across cultures. Hopefully, you recognize and appreciate the strengths you already have in these areas and are bolstering your self-confidence and spirit of resilience to move into more challenging cross-cultural personal growth activities.

In the next chapter, we will apply your cross-cultural know-how to your opportunities to influence the attitudes, behaviors, cooperation, and commitment of others to succeed in delivering results.

Three

Exercising Your Personal Influence and Persuasion

Now that we have laid a foundation of cultural know-how, we are ready to study various approaches to influence within a multicultural international setting. What you know about your audience will inform your selection of influence strategies. In this chapter we will explore a variety of strategies you might use to influence others. We'll look at what conditions might make one strategy work better than another. You will also find practical and proven methods, tools, and best practices to employ.

Big Picture Scan

Before you read on, answer these questions:

- Do you engage your target audiences' ability to reason when attempting to influence them?
- Do you persuade your audiences by using relational and emotional appeals?
- Do you have a simple fill-in-the-blank formula for developing a business case for your ideas and initiative to present to your audiences?
- Have you made a thorough list of the people you will want to influence in your steppingstone strategy?
- Do you know the personal self-interests and group interests of all of those on whom you will depend to deliver the expected results of your initiative?

- When you think of whom you will have to influence, do you imagine the most senior executives or beneficiaries of your initiative?

- Do you know who the MAD people are (those with the money, authority, and desire to enact your idea)?

- Do you know how you might adapt your influence strategy to the dimensions of culture of your target audiences?

- Do you take into account the pressures your audiences are under when determining your approach to influence them?

- When you think of the upside or benefits of your initiative, do you first consider the payoff to the individuals whose cooperation you will require?

Test the Theory with Your Reality

Now identify various situations in which you are engaged in influencing someone or some group of people. Keep your real-life challenges in mind as you read the next section. Test the theory and practice against your own experience.

In this chapter, we will introduce the science of personal influence and persuasion by describing the two routes to persuasion, important considerations for identifying who will be your targets in your influence steppingstone strategy, and a simple formula for developing a persuasive interest-based business case. We will illustrate the challenge that comes in accurately targeting the right audience and artfully using the appropriate strategy based on the audience's dimensions of culture, tolerance of pressure, and personal self-interests.

The Science of Personal Influence and Persuasion

The two routes to personal influence and persuasion are the central and peripheral.[1] The central route is the more rational approach. The peripheral is the more relational. This chapter discusses these two routes in relation to the audience's cultural values and practices and will provide important clues to which route you will want to lead with. Both the rational and relational approaches to persuasion and influence include strategies to effectively win the hearts and minds of your audience.

The Central Route to Influence

You are using the central route to influence others when you actively engage your listeners' thinking (cognition). You appeal to people's cognitive reasoning by proposing the merits of an issue using logic and evidence. You present a logical business case, outline the costs and benefits, and anticipate objections or counterarguments. A central or rational influence strategy results in a lasting or durable change in the listeners' attitudes because you have actively engaged their minds.

When does central influence work best? That depends on the dimensions of culture involved. For example, many people value and operate out of a performance- and task-oriented mind-set: stick to the facts, get to the truth, and state the case from the perspective of the advancement of mutual interests. When you want to get to business and come to agreement for the sake of the transaction, the rational approach to influence will be most effective. For those who are very "now" oriented and believe in cutting to the bottom line, you will want to state your case and lead with a central influence approach.

However, with people who are highly relationship oriented, the peripheral route to persuasion is the place to start. Where the culture values and emphasizes building a strong base of relationship, familiarity, credibility, and trust, your rational strategy will have to wait. Here, the relationship is first and the transaction is later—if the relationship is a fit.

Because the central influence strategy is a cognitive or rational approach to persuasion, your audience's readiness and ability to think are essential. The effectiveness of the central route to influence depends on three factors: the listeners' motivation to think, their ability to think, and the number of opportunities they will have to think about or repeat your message.

Your Listeners' Motivation to Think

Your listeners' motivation to think will depend on several factors. For some, this may begin with the firm foundation of a trusting relationship. In addition, when people see the relevance or personal significance of your idea or initiative to their lives, their team, their collective or individual goals, they will be more motivated to listen to the merits of your proposal. Your ability to draw a straight line from the goals of your initiative to the goals of your listeners—a clear line of sight—will capture their interest. When they realize their participation is consequential to the outcome of your initiative, they are likely to listen and engage their thinking. Another motivator is listeners' anticipation of being asked to debate, present, or discuss the topic at another time.

In a more hierarchical culture that expects and accepts power, status, and authority, you may need to refer to a formal mandate and "borrow" the formal authority of a subject-matter expert or upper management to motivate someone to listen. You borrow someone's authority when you refer to that person's name, title, and credentials. For example, you may say, "Vishnu Hagarthiwas, global general manager of our latest blockbuster product, Intuition," or "When I was working with so-and-so, she said this was appropriate."

Your Listeners' Ability to Think

You cannot take your listeners' ability to think for granted. For example, consider how distracted we all make ourselves with multitasking. You can facilitate your listeners' ability to think by paying attention to a number of conditions:

- *Attention:* If your audience is attentive and there are minimal distractions, your listeners will be more able to consider your proposal. So your job is to create a setting with minimal distractions.

- *Simplicity:* If your message is simple and easily understood, your listeners will be more open to think about and be persuaded by your proposal. Reinforce your idea's simplicity by keeping its key points to only a handful of items. People remember openings and closings, so be sure to repeat your simplified statement at the opening and closing of your spoken message. The litmus test here is your listeners' ability to repeat the key points in your absence.

■ *Written reinforcement:* When you provide a written message to accompany your spoken message, you will reinforce your message. When your listeners are able to see and read at their own pace, they will be more likely to understand and retain your message.

■ *Comprehensibility:* When your language is clear and concise and when your pace or rate of speech is reasonable, your message will be more easily understood. Your comprehensibility will help your listeners be more open to persuasion. (Remember Dr. Culture's machine in chapter 2.)

■ *Cultural compatibility:* When your message is consistent with the listeners' cultural perspectives, values, beliefs, and practices, they are less likely to raise objections and more likely to be open to persuasion. Ask yourself, "What *are* my listeners' existing beliefs? How does my message fit into their existing beliefs?"

Opportunities for Your Listeners to Think about Your Issue

When your listeners are presented with repeated opportunities to hear about your idea, on other meeting agendas, for example, they will think about your proposal again. As they hear a strong number of compelling, issue-related arguments and persuasive proof, they accumulate evidence that stacks up in favor of your position. Consider how you might create repeated opportunities for them to think about your message. Repeated exposure to your idea or initiative will reinforce your message and enhance your audience's memory and understanding.

In summary, the central route to persuasion works best when your audience is motivated to think about your issue, is able to think about your issue, and has repeated exposure to compelling evidence in favor of your initiative. Even without the authority to command and control others, you can prepare a setting and atmosphere in which your listeners are motivated and able to think about what you want to tell them. Doing what you can to control the circumstances of your conversation will prepare your listeners' brains.

Know that the central route to influencing change is the route that will endure. It has sticking power.

But what if you can't even get on people's calendars? When the topic or issue is not instantly or obviously relevant to people, a rational approach will not be immediately effective. When the central reason for your initiative or issue is not even on the radar of your listeners, you will want to send subtle signals to persuade your listeners without requiring them to think. This is the peripheral route to influence.

The Peripheral Route to Influence

The peripheral route to influence and persuasion takes place in the *absence* of thinking. Peripheral influence is based on subtle cues or signals present in the setting in which your personal interaction takes place but not central to the logic or evidence you provide. This type of influence still goes on in the brain but in the emotional center rather than the reasoning centers of the brain. To be effective, you will always want to balance the rational and relational influence routes. The route you take first may be determined by a variety of factors.

Peripheral influence is the route to take with people of cultures that are relationship first, transaction later. Rather than focusing on the issues of problems or opportunities and evidence to address and resolve those issues, peripheral influence uses minimal issue-related thinking. As a result, peripheral influence is much less durable than central influence. It requires constant reinforcement. For those who are more future and long-term oriented, this constant reinforcement is the making of a long-term relationship. You will always want to be prepared to complement your central, rational approach with the peripheral route to persuasion. Failure to focus on the relationship will defeat even the most logical position.

For example, business managers can expect to have long-term relationships with their national, regional, and local regulators. A fact of doing business is that you will be regulated and audited by some legal entity, whether it be financial, environmental, or governmental. The relationship can be nurtured and developed to smooth the process of difficult transactions, or it can be perceived as adversarial, ignored, and treated as a transaction to be completed as efficiently and effectively as possible. In one region of a multinational organization, two successive regional CEOs treated local and national regulators with disdain and rudeness. After years of enduring escalating arrogance and a tone of intellectual superiority and impatience, the head of the regulatory commission demanded that the global CEO fly into the regional regulatory meeting and escort the abrasive regional CEO out of the meeting. The regional CEO may have been able to treat internal subordinates with disdain, but the external business partnership, where the CEO's authority held no sway, would not tolerate the tone of this relationship, and the CEO was asked to resign. A just-the-facts central route to persuasion that dismisses the human side of a relationship is never effective. A balance must be struck and maintained for any long-term relationship to be successful.

When your audience represents relationship-first, long-term cultures, or when the initiative or issue is not obviously relevant to transaction-oriented listeners, you will want to lead with the peripheral route to persuasion.

Now you will be introduced to some powerful cues or signals you will want to send to your listeners and how you can take advantage of these powerful signals to win your listeners over.

Persuasion Signals to Send to Your Listeners

Figure 2 lists some of the most familiar signals or cues your listeners and observers receive that cue them to be persuaded—or dissuaded—by you. You will recognize many of them. Below is a reminder of the research finding for each of these signals, a question you might ask yourself before each influence opportunity, and suggestions for how you might send favorably persuasive signals to your audience.

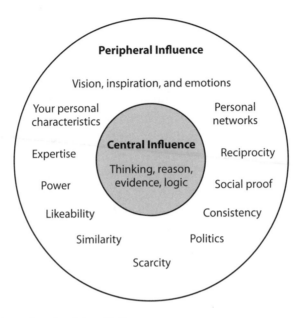

Figure 2 Examples of peripheral influence

- *Vision, inspiration, and emotions:* People respond to a sense of higher purpose, values, or beliefs. You are sending strong peripheral influence signals when you convey the higher purpose, values, and beliefs your initiative represents. A common misconception is that successful appeals laced with emotion, vision, and inspiration are best left to a small number of charismatic individuals born with some gift. On the contrary, it is a matter of knowing the value of such appeals and stating them truthfully. How might you highlight how your initiative contributes to the values and beliefs you share with your audience? You are using visionary persuasion when you make statements related directly to the values, vision, and purpose of each unique audience at the beginning and ending of your message. For example, you might state that being involved in your initiative has a larger significance for the business, the organization, customers, or society. Or you might say that involvement in this initiative could give the audience the chance to do important things very well, raise their own level of expertise, stretch themselves and their teams in their professional development, raise the bar for the kinds of work the organization takes on, or do what needs to be done by a higher standard than cost savings.

- *Personal networks:* People open doors and opportunities to friends and those with whom they have favorable relationships. Chapter 5 will deal with the importance of networks and connections in greater depth from the point of view of expanding your circle of relationships, gathering information, and discovering opportunities. From a peripheral influence perspective, existing favorable relationships with others will make those people inclined to support you whether or not they are particularly aware of or understand the relevance of your need. Can someone you know introduce you to the next person in your steppingstone strategy? You are influencing using the power of your network when you contact someone in your network for information that is difficult to access using formal channels of communication. When you give or receive resources difficult to acquire or at a discount, or when you ask for an introduction to a person you do not know personally, you are using the power of your personal network.

- *Reciprocity:* People of all cultures generally repay in kind, so give what you want to receive. However, do not wait for or expect others to follow your example.[2] Have you ever wanted or felt compelled to do for others who have done a favor for you? You are using the principle of persuasion through reciprocity whenever you go out of your way to do for others. Being aware of the resources you have that others may want will provide you with influence to leverage.

A strong working relationship is reciprocal. If, however, you give with the *expectation* of reciprocal treatment and are disappointed, your relationship may be tainted. So make your offers independent of any expectations to be repaid in kind. The goal of influencing others is to leave the relationship better with each personal and professional encounter. Waiting for or expecting the other person to reciprocate or to follow your example of giving is not productive. If you expect others to follow your lead and they do not, you may withhold future good deeds.

- *Social proof:* People follow the lead of others like them. You are influencing using the power of social proof, also commonly referred to as "peer pressure," when you talk about how other comparable businesses or groups your listeners esteem are moving ahead. Think about it. When was the last time you did something because you heard a competitor or colleague was doing it? Do you know whom your listeners consider a peer or a competitive equal? Investigate to find credible peers who are moving ahead in the same or similar direction you wish your listeners to move in, and tell them about these peers.

- *Consistency:* People do what they clearly commit to actively, voluntarily, and publicly. Being true to one's word and true to how one sees oneself is a strong motivator. When your listeners publicly declare their commitment to act in a way that demonstrates support for your initiative, and that requires some effort, they are much more likely to follow through than if they tell you in private or say nothing at all. Do you ask people throughout your meetings to state their commitments aloud or summarize comments in such a way as to gauge a statement of support? The goal is to ask them to volunteer to publicly state the actions they will take in support of your idea. Many international managers tell me that they have neglected the "requires some effort" part. They let the key people whose commitment they need get off the hook by only signing their names to endorse an initiative rather than tactfully engaging in a discussion of what that endorsement might look like. You are applying the principle of consistency when you discuss what the most effective use of one's endorsement looks like and how that same kind of endorsement might be applied to your initiative.

- *Politics:* People and groups use their decision-making power to support the agendas of those who understand, support, and align themselves with their own agendas. This is a bit like reciprocity and the political adage "You scratch my back; I'll scratch yours." In a large or complex organization, decisions are often made in favor of groups with the most visibility and critical mass of support. You are using the power of political influence when you understand how decisions are made and align yourself with groups with popular initiatives or individual "rising stars." Are you aware of popular initiatives that complement yours? As we said in chapter 1, political savvy is knowing how to use the influence of others to get things done. The goal is to align your initiative with related initiatives or like-minded groups that are moving in the same direction as your initiative to create a greater mass of support. In this way you use the momentum of others whenever possible.

- *Scarcity:* People want things that are not widely available, they can't have, or they feel they are in danger of having less of than someone else. The limited availability of something tangible or intangible—time, money, status, or material objects, for example—only serves to make that thing more desirable. Where do you hold scarce resources that others might need? You are using the influence power of scarcity when you emphasize that a good, service, rate, or decision you are offering is open and available only for a certain period or under limited conditions.

Your Personal Characteristics

In addition to the signals that cue an audience to be persuaded, people are open to persuasion based on the personal characteristics or attributes of the person who is trying to persuade them. Different cultures respond to these characteristics differently, so you need to be familiar with your own personal characteristics. In this way you will be aware of when your personal characteristics are likely to work for you or against you in your efforts to persuade. Below are a number of characteristics you will want to use as sources of influence power.

- *Expertise:* People accept and defer to the opinions of recognized experts. When in doubt, members of all cultures are more likely to be open to persuasion if they know you are an expert or authority in some respect. You are using your influence power when you make certain your expertise, experience, or education on a subject is known by those you seek to persuade. A common error is to assume your audience is already aware of your authority.

  You may ask someone you know in the group you wish to influence what he or she *thinks* would establish your credibility most quickly with this group. One way to make your authority most conspicuous is to tell your audience of your background, expertise, experience, or education. However, some cultures consider talking about yourself immodest. Have you ever neglected to share your expertise due to personal modesty or disdain for self-promoters? If this is the case, ask the person who is making your introduction if he or she would be willing to say a few words about your expertise or experience as part of your introduction.

  Remember that if you are unknown to the group you are trying to influence, people will do a web search for information about you. So it is important to do a web search yourself first to see what they will find.

- *Power:* Your formal position power, status as a decision maker, or relationship with those with power, fame, or wealth is a strong source of personal influence. This is particularly true with members of cultures that expect and accept that power is distributed unequally and defer to those with power as discussed in chapter 2. The sense of being close to the center of where important decisions are made is very attractive to many people and can be used as a source of influence. You are using your personal power with these people when you refer to your title, connections, wealth of resources, or span of control; offer exclusive information about people they consider important; or offer them the opportunity to see and to be seen by people they consider important.

For example, in an international matrix organization, employees nearer the bottom or middle of the organization may have only one manager or two managers—one solid-line and one dotted-line manager. Those at the top have many more internal stakeholders and dotted lines of accountability. In a meeting of one of the largest businesses in a multinational organization, the members of the executive committee were competing during a break about who had the most dotted-line accountabilities: "I have five," "Well, I have six," and so on. Symbols of power and status abound in every organization.

The significance of power is viewed alternatively by members of some cultures. They believe inequalities among people should be minimized and are not impressed by formal status and privileges. "They put their pants on the same way I do" is a common refrain. You are using your influence power with these people when you deliberately play down or disregard your formal title, status, wealth, privileges, importance, or connection to people with power.

- *Likability:* Research proves repeatedly that people like those who like them. If members of your audience like you, you will have a jump-start in persuading them. I often work with individuals who do not like or respect their managers or the person whose cooperation they require to get results. They hit roadblocks at every turn trying to influence the decisions of individuals they do not like. If you do not like the people you need to influence, you will be fighting an uphill battle in your attempts to influence them. If you hate your boss or a coworker because he or she has betrayed you in some way, I suggest you find ways to forgive and release the betrayal. You will do your initiative and your team no good by being right. This is so much easier said than done.

But if a relationship of trust and respect is a fundamental prerequisite to doing business in more than half the world's population, it is worth trying. You are using the influence power of likability when you offer genuine praise whenever possible. I often say that "tact" is telling others what you know they already think about themselves. Uncover the positive qualities your listeners believe they embody and those you wish they did and draw attention to these.

Failure to like and be liked is risky business. Do you believe you can give and earn respect by acting in a trustworthy manner without conveying dislike in your tone and facial expression? Do you believe that simply not liking another individual does not make you adversaries? Keep in mind that not displaying dislike and genuinely liking someone are two very different feelings. You are using the power of likability when you partner with someone your audience does like and can warm to.

- *Similarity:* People like those who are similar to them. People are more likely to be persuaded by you if you look like, sound like, and talk like them. The converse is also true. For some, different is dangerous because it is often unknown. Extreme differences can cause extreme anxiety. We have learned that some cultures avoid uncertainty and others tolerate it as a matter of course. You are using the influence power of similarity when you uncover similar or related interests. You may not enjoy the immediate benefits of relational or peripheral persuasion with people who are not like you, whose demographics are very different from yours—your age, race, ethnicity, gender, education, income, and language, for example—especially if they have a negative bias against the demographics you represent. This makes the discovery of common interests extremely important.

  A business manager from Canada did not trust his Russian manager, with whom he believed he had nothing in common. Their values, their priorities, their decision-making styles—everything was at odds. Knowing his distrust and these differences were harming his chances of influencing his manager's decisions, the Canadian manager set about exploring interests he and his manager had in common. He discovered they were both passionate about ice hockey. He bought two tickets to an important ice hockey game and invited his manager. They did no more than shout and drink beer and enjoy the game together, but the mutual effort and passion helped forge a bond. As a result, they no longer automatically opposed each other and began to listen to one another with greater respect.

Think back to a time when you uncovered similarities with someone you needed to influence. How often did you both refer to those common interests? Whom do you need to influence and know you will really need to dig to uncover common ground with? Your ability to genuinely like or find similarities with someone else is possible when you decide in advance to do so. It's a mind-set.

Aristotle and the Art of Persuasion

Aristotle called persuasion an "art" and urged the use and balance of three key elements: the audience's emotions, or "pathos"; the talk's logic and reasoning, or "logos"; and the speaker's credibility or "ethos."[3] Logos is the equivalent of the central or rational route to persuasion. Ethos and pathos combine to align with the peripheral or relational route to persuasion.

The personal character or ethos of a speaker can induce listeners to believe in the speaker in advance of the presentation of any proof. When you succeed in establishing credibility and inspire the trust of your audience, you have greater power to persuade.

Pathos refers to your ability to put the audience in a certain frame of mind and appeal to the emotions of the listeners. You must know them well in order to effectively appeal to their emotions—anger, sorrow, happiness, fear, scorn—and to produce these emotions within the course of your persuasive communication.

Finally, when you use logic, present compelling evidence, and seek to prove a truth, this is logos.

Aristotle's discourse on persuasion reminds us that in order to effectively influence, you need to keep all three elements in focus and in balance. And Aristotle came to this same conclusion without the benefit of years of multidisciplinary research we have today to prove the point about central and peripheral influence.

CASE STUDY
Zainab Salbi and the Art of Persuasion

A wonderful example of this blend of ethos, pathos, and logos is from a 2010 speech by Iraqi-born Zainab Salbi, who founded Women for Women International, an organization that calls for having women at the negotiating table to build lasting and sustainable peace.[4]

Salbi began by establishing her personal credibility to speak about war with a vivid illustration of her firsthand experience of war as a citizen of Iraq. She described how she felt as she saw bombs explode outside her bedroom window. She then shifted to her emotional appeal: "We have been so consumed with seemingly objective discussions of politics, tactics, weapons, dollars, and casualties. This is the language of sterility. How casually we treat casualties [of war]." Here she pulled in the listeners personally by using the pronoun "we," not pointing her finger and distancing herself from the listeners as "you" but including the audience with her.

Having established her credibility and appealed to the listeners' emotions and values, she shifted to her compelling evidence. "Eighty percent of refugees around the world are women and children. . . . Ninety percent of modern war casualties are civilians—75 percent of them are women and children. . . . Half a million women in Rwanda get raped in one hundred days. Or, as we speak, hundreds and thousands of Congolese women are getting raped and mutilated. How interesting. These just become numbers we refer to." Salbi led with her personal authority as a credible eyewitness (ethos) and her peripheral influence by appealing to the emotions of her audience (pathos). In this way, Salbi created a connection with her audience that set the stage for a central or cognitive appeal using facts of very vivid evidence (logos). Zainab Salbi may vary her approach based on her audience, but she has all the elements to set the stage and build her case for change.

The need for rational (central route) and relational (peripheral route) persuasion has been proven by research, validated by one of the most influential philosophers regarding the art of persuasion, and illustrated in a persuasive presentation to an international forum. Knowing your audience will guide you in achieving the proper balance of these two routes to successfully influence.

With these two critical influence tools in hand, you are better equipped for your journey on your steppingstone strategy.

Clarifying Your Influence Objective

Each influence journey begins with a clear picture of your ultimate goal, the destination. Toward this end, you will take a series of small moves to progress along your influence steppingstone strategy. Each step will have a particular, intermediate goal.

For example, your intermediate persuasion goals may be as mundane and pragmatic as the following:

- I want to persuade D to introduce me to B.

- I want to sufficiently inform and prepare X to inform and persuade Y.

- I want to establish a regular schedule of contacts with G to build a relationship and to eventually gain access to G's network of connections within C organization.

- I want to inspire F with our vision in order to gain F's interest.

- I want to reframe E's perception of what we do in XYZ in order to establish our credibility.

- I want to listen to and understand the interests of M as a foundation for a lasting relationship.

- I want to impress and surprise L with our current and anticipated future performance results so L will consider lending subject-matter experts to our effort.

These are just a few examples of the kinds of goals you will want to achieve in your influence steppingstone strategy. Your effectiveness in delivering results depends on your ability to set and meet task and relationship goals that are both short- and long-term.

Knowing Your Audience

To achieve your objective and arrive at your destination at the end of your influence efforts, you must know which route to take. In some cases you will lead with your heart; in others you will lead with your head. Knowing which route to take—whether relational or rational— begins with a thorough understanding of your audience. For example, from a cross-cultural perspective, we know the central or cognitive route appeals initially to the more performance-oriented cultures and the peripheral or relational route appeals initially to the more relationship-oriented cultures. Your cross-cultural know-how will help answer the questions, "Will this audience need and expect to build a relationship with me over time before engaging in a rational discussion of costs and benefits? Or will this audience expect me to cut to the chase, state the bottom line up front, and be prepared to prove the truth of my claims with clear and concise evidence?"

Influence begins with knowing your audience.

Identify Your Target Audiences

Who *is* your target audience? Who has the greatest influence in deciding the fate of your initiative? And working backward, whom do you have to influence to get to that final approval? It is surprising how many people do not consider these all-important questions. Whom do you most need to influence—one step at a time?

Because you are influencing within a complex international matrix organization, the vast majority of decisions are shared within two or more functional, business, regional, or global reporting lines. As discussed previously, having a clear line of sight from the goal of your initiative to the goals of the organization is important. Your checkerboard steppingstone strategy is designed to identify those who influence or share decision making along the way to your ultimate goal. If you have decided to target those at a layer below the ultimate decision makers—people who are most likely to be consulted before making a decision—you will need to learn exactly who they are.

EXPECT A CHANGING CAST OF CHARACTERS
Shifting Decision-Making Power and Authority

Who has the greatest influence in deciding the fate of your initiative? That depends.

Within a complex, multidimensional matrix organization, it is challenging to identify who most influences what decisions. In chapter 1, we discussed the complexity of the multidimensional matrix organization that is structured to share functional expertise with the business units, as well as leverage local regional customer relationships and product or service delivery outlets.

We also discussed the importance of identifying the person or persons who influence the decision makers rather than targeting the busy decision makers themselves. In chapter 5 we will discuss how to use your network and the networks of others to connect to those you will need and want to influence. However, it is useful to have some concept of how decision-making authority may be distributed as a starting point.

For example, business unit general managers and functional executives who determine which resources are required where and coordinate the redistribution of resources may have more influence than the regional manager. Where similar resources are expected to be shared across regional borders, in order to reduce the costs of duplication of resources across all regions, one region or country may house a Center of Excellence (COE). A Center of Excellence is appointed because of its regional supply of natural resources, technology, or workers with the talent, experience, and expertise to draw on as demand increases. For example, Dow Chemical has an engineering center in China because of that area's concentration of a vast number of engineers, who serve the company's global manufacturing business. A Center of Excellence develops global scale and expertise and is responsible for creating the supply to meet cross-border demands and for constant innovation in its area of expertise.

If, on the other hand, the highest income-generating customers are concentrated in one region or country, a region or country man-·ager may have significant influence.

Expect the popularity, authority, and resources of even the most senior executives to change with some regularity. International matrix organizations are designed to shift with changes in the local, regional, and global economy, market, social attitudes, tax policy, civic unrest, or government regulations. For example, one regional build-out may be put on hold as another, more predictable or emerging region is emphasized.

Target Audience: Questions to Consider

We have previously discussed the importance of remembering that you are strategically positioning your initiative—not yourself. However, as we have seen, you must build many trusting relationships. You will not achieve your initiative without others, and members of your team will represent the initiative as well. As the faces of this initiative, you and your team will want to be sure you are all on the same page about the relationships of cooperation required and the influence targets that are being won as the project rolls out.

As you plot your influence strategy, you will be identifying whose cooperation, political capital, and social connections you will need. Keep in mind the law of equifinality: "There is more than one way to skin a cat." There is no one best way.[5] With the help of your team brainstorm a set of questions to target those you will need to win over in your influence planning efforts. For example, who currently shares the decision-making authority, budget, similar vision, or status you seek to influence within the *formal* organizational hierarchy? What specific connections and relationships does your target audience have to better position your initiative? Does your audience have access to exclusive information; close relationships with highly connected others; control of large programs, employee bases, and budgets; a charismatic, enthusiastic, or visionary personality; and intelligence?

These and other questions will help guide you in targeting the right audiences to influence. The strength of your strategic positioning and your personal network will complement your ability to influence and persuade when it comes to identifying your influence targets.

Your Audience's Audience

In a complex international organization, where decisions affect overlapping budgets and interests, experience will tell you to expect a time-consuming decision-making process involving multiple people you will need to influence. You may be able to identify everyone whose input and agreement will be needed to make a decision in your favor, but you cannot assume you will have a relationship with or be known by everyone. For these reasons, you will need to depend on the depth and breadth of relationships within your network, the network of your team, and the connections of your network's network—the constellation effect discussed in chapter 5. Part of your influence steppingstone strategy is to persuade your audience to influence the audiences with whom they have established relationships. Your message will be repeated by someone else (or several others) until you reach the ultimate decision makers. This means your message must contain evidence and emotional appeal that will sway a variety of audiences along the path to agreement. Your message must also be sufficiently clear and concise to be repeated consistently and accurately as it goes from audience to audience.

Cultural Dimensions and Influence

To influence successfully across a multicultural international organization, you will need to observe, identify, and understand your audience's dimensions of culture. Your organization's culture may be so strong that individual cultures may be subsumed. However, in the case of a decentralized international corporation where regions had been given complete autonomy for decades, it is not safe to assume all regions will adopt the one-culture DNA overnight.

When you understand each audience has a mosaic of cultural dimensions, you are more likely to broaden your influence strategy. Using the same dimensions of culture described in chapter 2, figure 3 describes different influence strategies that might be used for different dimensions of culture.

THE ART OF THE INTEREST-BASED BUSINESS CASE
The Push-Pull-How Influence Strategy

One of the most powerful tools in the global manager's tool kit is a simple and straightforward formula for a persuasive business case. Once you are armed with an appreciation for the rationale and complexities of a matrix organization, a cross-cultural mind-set, a knowledge of the rational and relational approaches to influence, and the keys to building lasting commitment, all that remains is a plug-and-play business case formula.

If you don't have a simple and memorable formula, you can waste time in reinventing the wheel and lose opportunities to present your business case that arise in the moment. Whether you have weeks to prepare a presentation to a board or an opportunity to think on your feet, you need to have an easy-to-remember, three-point, fill-in-the-blank formula for your persuasive business case.

The simple formula on page 120 has been proven effective by hundreds of leaders of all levels and cultures in international organizations. Once you are familiar with this interest-based business case, you will begin to recognize it in the speeches, discussions, and presentations of the leaders you most admire.

Creating a business case does not have to be complicated. In fact, the easier the formula is to remember, the more confident you will be that all your bases are covered and the more motivated you will be to engage in influencing others.

COMMON INTERPERSONAL DILEMMA TO RECONCILE **Approach to Teamwork**	
Individualistic ←——— CULTURAL DIMENSION ———→ *Collectivistic*	
Uses "I." Stresses individual accountability, freedom, independence, and mobility. Emphasizes personal objectives and interests. Is a self-starter, takes initiative, and completes tasks without direction. Takes credit. Expresses admiration of individual achievement. Looks after self and immediate family.	Uses "we." Does not call attention to oneself. Emphasizes group interdependence, accountability, loyalty, and commitment. Allows interests of group to prevail. Gives top priority to the good of the whole rather than the individual. Shares resources and credit. Considers direct confrontation rude and undesirable. Believes social network is primary. Encourages and rewards group action and distribution of resources. Expresses pride in and admiration of group achievement.
←——— INFLUENCE CONSIDERATIONS ———→	
Emphasize how your initiative promotes people's self-interests and contributes to the goals of their initiatives and performance scorecards. Highlight the possibilities of acting autonomously. Be prepared to demonstrate how the success of your initiative will bring people visibility and positive recognition and rewards.	Emphasize how your initiative contributes to the overall interests of the team, unit, or group. Explicitly state the connection to the company strategy and common group or team goals. Highlight the impact on interdependencies. Demonstrate how your initiative and their initiatives complement each other, overlap, and require mutual success and interdependence. Use the pronoun "we." Encourage and reward collective group action and distribution of resources.

COMMON INTERPERSONAL DILEMMA TO RECONCILE **Significance of Power and Status**	
Egalitarianism ←——— CULTURAL DIMENSION ———→ *Hierarchy*	
Interacts without overt recognition of power and status. Managers are consultative. Employees prefer being consulted. Employees resist dependence on managers, will contradict them, and will be emotional, friendly, and informal with managers.	Recognizes power, status, and hierarchy. Expects and accepts that power is distributed unequally. Consults with and supports initiatives of superiors. Managers use authoritarian or paternalistic style, providing for employees' needs but without great freedom or responsibilities, which employees prefer. Employees depend on bosses, are afraid of or are unlikely to openly disagree with them or to be emotional or familiar with them.

Significance of Power and Status continues on next page

Figure 3 Cultural dimensions and behavior, dilemmas, and influence considerations

Significance of Power and Status	
Underscore employee buy-in.	Recall an executive mandate and approval to cooperate, collaborate, and complete your initiative.
Create opportunities to solicit employee input.	
Emphasize employee initiative. Ask employees to volunteer to take initiative.	State the names and titles of important and well-known executives aligned with this initiative.
Encourage intellectual exploration, brainstorming, and creativity.	Emphasize the negative consequences of acting outside the mandates of senior management.
	Make assignments, make statements, and avoid bargaining.

COMMON INTERPERSONAL DILEMMA TO RECONCILE **Importance of Task versus Relationship**	
Performance and task oriented (low context) ◄─── CULTURAL DIMENSION ───►	*Cooperation and relation-ship oriented (high context)*
Is direct. Asserts opinion. Appears stern. Believes in importance of transactions, tasks, and facts first. May appear loud and interrupts others. Appears self-assured and may appear arrogant. Appears to act regardless of cues in the setting, i.e., low context or situational awareness. Is competitive. Strives to win. Creates opportunities for personal advancement, higher earnings, and recognition. Accepts conflict and confrontation.	Is indirect. Listens for cues in the setting about how to adapt tone and behavior, i.e., high context. Emphasizes relationship first, transaction later. Desires to please. Strives to have good relationship with direct superior, cooperative relationships with coworkers, and high quality of life. Strives for win-win solution. Resists standing out. Is modest.
◄─── INFLUENCE CONSIDERATIONS ───►	
Speak directly and get to the point. Present the business case in group forum. Present the bottom line first—impact on revenue, costs, and results in measurable terms.	Be prepared to establish relationships in advance of any discussion of a transaction. Wait for others to initiate the discussion of business. Observe cues in setting about how to proceed.
Call attention to what the competition is doing and how your initiative compares.	
Prepare for open debate of issues.	Discover common interests, uncover genuine liking, and offer genuine praise.
Emphasize your personal expertise and authority.	Emphasize your personal approachability and authenticity and the potential for harmony.
Speak crisply and use direct eye contact. Avoid qualifying or hedging statements.	Be prepared to meet and speak one-on-one to build agreement and consensus outside direct group exposure.
Emphasize excellence and performance improvements.	Highlight integrity, honesty, and sincerity.
	Be modest and self-effacing.

Figure 3 (continued)

COMMON INTERPERSONAL DILEMMA TO RECONCILE **Communication**	
Accuracy, uncertainty avoidance ⟵ CULTURAL DIMENSION ⟶	*Diplomacy, ambiguity tolerance*
Highly values explicit truth and accuracy. Feels the threat of the unknown. Prefers predictability. Prefers rules—written and unwritten. Openly discusses people, events, things, and inner feelings. Overtly strives for accuracy and precision in communication.	Believes everything is relative. Says, "It depends." Desires harmony in communication and relationships. Is sensitive to the feelings and reputations of others. Gives and expects to receive bad news in private. Is open to innovation and uncertainty.
⟵ INFLUENCE CONSIDERATIONS ⟶	
Make statements of fact and provide compelling evidence. Use quantitative data. Alleviate the stress of the unpredictable. Emphasize the reliance on policies, social norms, rituals, and bureaucratic procedures. Emphasize an orderly, systematic, and organized plan.	Prepare to offer a variety of key considerations and dependencies upon which success depends. Emphasize bargaining and a win-win outcome. Accentuate a worldly wise and diplomatic approach.

COMMON INTERPERSONAL DILEMMA TO RECONCILE **Orientation to Time**	
Short term, sequential ⟵ CULTURAL DIMENSION ⟶	*Long term, synchronistic*
Is past and present oriented. Handles one thing at a time. Is highly conscious of time, is schedule driven, starts and stops on time, and is task driven. Takes deadlines seriously. Is aware of constraints of others' time and becomes frustrated and impatient with missed deadlines and late starts. Prefers immediate gratification.	Is future oriented. Handles many things at once. Is less conscious of time, adheres less to schedule or punctuality. Understands emerging time requirements and is sensitive to others' workloads. Invests resources in the long term at the expense of immediate results. Prefers delayed gratification.
⟵ INFLUENCE CONSIDERATIONS ⟶	
Emphasize the positive impact on time savings, adherence to the current schedule, and urgency of making agreed-upon deadlines. Highlight the costs of delay. Accentuate the savings and opportunities of acting now. Stress the benefits and immediate results.	Underscore the impact on future sustainability. Emphasize how the costs of today's investment will improve future results. Accentuate the visionary nature of the plan, foresight, and strategic planning. Prove long-term payoffs and sustainability for future generations.

Figure 3 (continued)

You can use these three influence strategies as the basis of your business case:

- The push: create a dire picture of the present status quo.
- The pull: create a compelling and desirable future vision.
- The how: provide a credible and feasible strategy for achieving that future.

The Push: What's Wrong with the Status Quo?

The first step in developing a persuasive business case is to provide a compelling reason *why* change is necessary. What will happen if we don't change? This requires a clear description of the present situation and its consequences. You will create interest in your message by stating in bold terms the dire consequences of doing business as usual. What do we stand to lose if we stay with the status quo? "Loss language" like this is a strong motivator.

This influence strategy operates on the concept of increasing pressure to create a personal sense of urgency. If a difference exists between the performance you want and the performance you are getting today, how big is that gap and how long can you tolerate it? If there is stagnation and absence of momentum, the current state is just not painful enough. Or the pain or dissatisfaction has persisted for so long it has become a part of the environment that has been collectively tolerated or accepted as a situation that cannot be overcome. A solid push is needed to overcome inaction. This requires a clear understanding of the consequences of doing nothing from the personal vantage point of your peers, team members, stakeholders, or business partners.

As a leader who influences change, you will sell the problem using convincing and strong statements with evidence your audience is most likely to find persuasive. To create a shared sense of urgency, stress the time sensitivity of your business case. Calculate the actual loss and costs of business as usual (in the currency the audience deals in), lost opportunity, or lost customers as each minute, day, or week passes. The current situation is dire. Act now.

The Pull: What Are the Benefits Individually and Collectively?

With pull language, you seek to attract audience members by explaining how they will benefit from your proposed solution. This influence strategy is the corollary to push. Whatever dire circumstances you introduce in the push you now counter or overcome with your pull. Again, provide statements of evidence your audience will find compelling. Speak personally to your audience's dreams and motivations. Do not simply say how this initiative benefits the company. Describe how your solution is customized to fulfill people's personal vision, self-interests, goals, and hopes.

Individual and Collective Interests

In addition to grounding your initiative in the organization's interests goals and vision, you will want to confirm your initiative appeals to individual and collective personal interests. Your audience analysis will include uncovering what the members value most from a personal and group perspective. Ask and listen carefully to learn if some of the items below are personal or group priorities of your audience.

- *Quality of work life:* How might your initiative have an impact on the work-life balance? Will it in any way improve people's quality of work life by increasing their participation or say in decisions that directly impact them?

- *Personal and collective performance:* Will your initiative positively and measurably impact the achievement of personal, team, and group performance goals? If so, how?

- *Peace of mind or reassurance:* How does your idea or initiative reduce personal anxieties (e.g., job security, personal safety, professional job qualifications) while maintaining sufficiently high levels of performance?

- *Challenge and learning:* How does work on this project present opportunities to learn, stretch, and grow professionally or intellectually?

- *Increased income:* What is the potential impact of your initiative on personal income, benefits, rewards, and bonus eligibility?

- *Personal or group exposure:* How might involvement in your initiative favorably impact personal or group exposure, visibility, recognition, and rewards?

When you have identified your initiative's line of sight with the goals and interests of the organization and the personal and collective interests of your audience, you can use this information as ingredients to create interest in your initiative and capture the attention of your audience.

Push + Pull = Why Change?

Together, push and pull provide the foundation of the interest-based business case. To make a strong business case, you need to answer the question, "Why change?" Your answer will include selling points based on the common interests you have identified—for example, values, vision, cost, revenue, performance, and so on.

Your claims of push and pull cannot stand on their own. They must be backed up with proof. Of all your evidence to support your claims, you will want to select the evidence your listeners are most likely to find persuasive. This customization of evidence depends on how well you know your audience and what standards of proof your listeners need and expect. Your evidence will illustrate just how severe today's problem really is with numbers and examples that support your push statements. When you maintain that your listeners will benefit (your pull statements), you can prove each claim with stories, data, and examples of measurable successes reached elsewhere with a similar initiative. Avoid generalities.

Think from your listeners' perspective: what evidence will be relevant to them and will they need to be convinced of the urgency and personal and collective benefits of your initiative?

- *Attachment to a higher purpose:* Show how your initiative is connected to a higher purpose. For example, an executive recently said about his initiative, "We have a double bottom line. Not only are we the most efficient, we fulfill the highest purpose of our mission: We treat children like citizens, not just consumers. We touch children's lives and make a difference. We offer rich content that is fun with characters that draw children in and have been endorsed by the national department of education."[6]

- *Return on investment:* What is the investment you recommend, and what kind of return do you expect? If you are speaking to an audience with a long-term orientation, you will want to emphasize the range and variety of future returns your initiative entails in a five-, ten-, or twenty-year horizon. Conversely, if you are speaking to listeners with a short-term orientation, you will want to emphasize payoffs in the next quarter or by the end of the first year.

- *Data-based statistics:* Consider the kind of specific data your listeners use to measure success. Water quality? Adaptability? Numbers of students enrolled? Reduction of infectious diseases? Net interest margin? New customer acquisition? Quality of work life? Community good will? What measure might you use to demonstrate improvement? Be prepared to prove how your initiative is a leading cause of these improvements.

- *Credible peer comparisons or social proof:* Prove your claim by citing credible peer competitors' activities and results. Use the highest industry standards and studies of the research firms highly regarded by this audience.

- *Relative proof:* Now make your data more vivid. Present your data in relative terms. For example, "The cost of one orphan's cot is equal to a year's worth of café latte." "This represents savings equal to 1,500 new accounts." "This time savings is worth 1 percent improvement in unemployment." "Our technology save is greater than the gross domestic product of many emerging nations."

- *Evaluative benchmarks:* Benchmarks are meaningful measures of an event in the present or the current state (e.g., the duration of a process, the average cost of shipping, the numbers of households receiving care). Provide today's benchmark and explain how an identical measure will be taken at a specified date in the future to prove the impact of your initiative.

- *Testimonials and real-life examples:* One of the most evocative and powerful of all proofs is a true story that illustrates your claim. If you claim your initiative will improve overall health, quality of life, or ease of use, can you provide favorable reports from others who will be recognized and respected by your audience? Tell a brief story that vividly illustrates the truth of your claims.

- *Experiential demonstrations and tangible objects:* Arrange an activity for your audience to experience what you are talking about firsthand. How might you provide a live demonstration or illustration for your listeners to see, touch, or hear your proof?

Your selection of proof that is relevant to your audience is essential. Together your push and pull answer the question, "Why change?" with evidence that is relevant to your audience—they form your business case. You need a careful balance of a meaningful push to exert pressure painful enough to move away from the present and a pull of attractive payoffs to compel forward movement. The push proves a problem exists and the danger of continuing to do things the way we do them now. The pull illustrates the benefits of the results you will deliver when your initiative is implemented. This leaves your listeners teetering on the brink of a transition from the present to the future. Their next logical question is, "How?"

The How: How Do We Reach Our Vision?

The third leg of this influence strategy, how, offers your approach to resolving the current dilemma and must assure your audience it will lead to your promised future state. Your message must persuade your audience that your course of action is the clear choice among other alternative routes. The how describes your plan for achieving the pull. It is the outline of your proposed solution that describes the strategy, goals, values, and behaviors that must be put in place to reach the pull. Further, your how broadly outlines the supporting mechanisms that will reinforce your approach, such as the organizational structure, policies and procedures, performance measures and incentives, and necessary skill development needed to stabilize, institutionalize, and sustain the changes as the new normal. Concrete goals and measures of progress and outcomes are also presented.

Your how plan addresses questions about key dependencies—time involved, employee resource requirements, skills training, and maintenance and support requirements. Those you wish to influence will expect you to present estimates of the time and level of effort your proposal will take, its costs, its impact on performance (including delays or accelerations), the near- and long-term results your proposal will generate.

How will you manage the transition and develop sustainability? Sustainability, as we discussed in chapter 1, takes into consideration more than the present challenges of the organization within the current environment. From an organizational perspective, sustainability means planning and implementing solutions that meet today's requirements and will not compromise the stability and health of the organization and its resources in future generations. A sustainable initiative is one that does not deplete resources faster than they can be regenerated. A plan is sustainable when it takes into account the impact it will have on the human social systems within an organization, the customers it serves, and the societies in which it operates. This is strategic thinking and planning.

Expect and plan for objections that will surface during the course of your how discussion. Concerns about risks, costs, the capacity to deliver, and the goodness of other approaches will all be debated. Your scan of the audience, your scan of the internal organization trends, and your strategic positioning resources will prepare you to address these concerns.

Promote Participation in the How to Influence Commitment
While you are describing the how, be aware that you are discussing a fairly high-level outline, which touches on details only as an

illustration of how your idea will be executed. Keep in mind that in any change effort, people support what they help to create. Creating engagement and buy-in requires the participation, input, and collaboration of the group that will be responsible for executing the solution. Offering the opportunity to have a say in building the solution can be designed and facilitated to maximize creative thinking, participation, and quality decision making.

Maintain a Mind-Set of Equifinality

"Equifinality" means there are many ways to achieve the same end. Once the goal is clarified and agreed upon, open the approach to the group and guide the process. It is not useful to quibble over changes in approach, even if this means you will lose complete ownership of what may have been your original idea. Sharing ownership will get the job done, although the method of arrival may be very different from what you imagined. When you increase the commitment of others, you decrease the burden you must carry on your own to deliver results.

Using Influence to Drive Change

Finally, this push-pull-how influence strategy mirrors organizational change theory. The earliest research in organizational development still serves as the major source of concepts and methods for leading organizational change. Broadly speaking, in order for organizations to change, the structures, policies, and systems that maintain the status quo must be reduced or eliminated. This is accomplished by presenting information—a business case—that demonstrates precisely how the current state or business as usual contradicts the desired future state.[7]

Figure 4 presents a familiar illustration of change theory. To influence organizational change, an urgent push out of the current state destroys the possibilities and complacency of the current state. Presenting an irrefutable picture of the present state in stark contrast with the desired, attractive pull or future vision of the organization is the critical first step to change. Destroy the current state and going back to business as usual is impossible. Forward energy and direction are motivated with a compelling picture of the future, which provides the unknown transition period with a future purpose. To persuade your listeners that you can lead and manage the transition from the present to a sustainable future, your how must outline a strategy that quickly sets up temporary structures to support the transition, promises successes along the way, and aligns with organizational, collective, and personal interests. Your journey story from the present to the future provides a meaningful and memorable image and inspires the confidence of your listeners in their ability to execute the change required. Your journey story will also identify you as a leader.

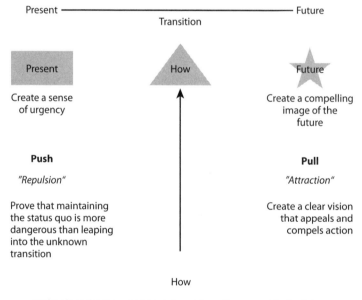

Outline broad actions and goals to get from the present to the future.

Figure 4 The "push-pull-how" model: Using influence to drive change

When Do You Use These Influence Strategies?

You may be wondering, "Do I have to use all three of these influence strategies, the push, the pull, and the how?" The answer requires some tolerance for ambiguity: it depends. As you cross international borders, cultures, and interests, you will want to customize your influence strategy based in part on the pressure the audience is experiencing.

Customize Pressure

We have already noted the impact of time pressure on how personal dimensions of culture will emerge over and above a strong organizational culture. Pressure also affects performance—both positively and negatively.

Studies show personal performance improves with pressure. Pressure arouses our interest and attention, excites centers in our brain that cause us to act, stimulates mental acuity and resourcefulness, and as a result, improves our level of performance. These studies find there is a level of pressure that is appropriate and optimum for each of us. This means that with too little pressure, your level of performance will stagnate. But as the pressure increases, your performance improves. With the right amount of pressure for you, you will eventually perform at your highest level. If the pressure continues to increase beyond what is right for you, it will have a hyperactive or panic effect and your performance will begin to diminish.

Another finding of this research is that the higher your skill in an area of performance, the greater amount of pressure you can tolerate in that particular arena. So one-size-fits-all pressure cannot be applied to individuals because they vary in their skill levels. Another finding states that different types of tasks (physical, mental, emotional) affect optimum levels of pressure for everyone. For example, if a job is intellectually or cognitively challenging and the performer must concentrate, less pressure is required or can be tolerated. If the job requires endurance or persistence, more pressure can be tolerated.[8]

The Drone Zone, the Stretch Zone, and the Panic Zone

This continuum of pressure from too little to too much creates three zones. (See figure 5.) The area of low pressure and low performance is the "drone zone." The point of highest performance, where the pressure is optimum, is the "stretch zone." The area where the pressure becomes too high and performance begins to diminish is the "panic zone." Pressure combined with operating outside one's skill or experience level or having to think under pressure will diminish performance. The pressure that sends one person into the drone zone could arouse someone else to stretch.

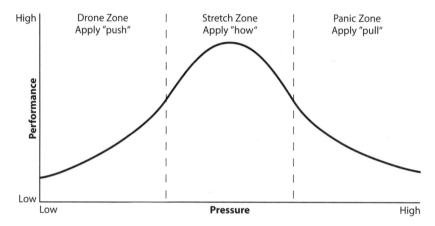

Figure 5 Know what "pressure" your listener is under

Stress research demonstrates the accumulated impact of multiple stressors. Even if I am feeling well within my depth professionally, as unexpected events or "fires" accumulate at work and in my personal life, the pressure shows up in my performance.

Apply this science to your art of persuasion and customize the pressure you exert to influence behavior. Emphasize push for an underperforming team. If members of your target audience are being complacent, acting entitled, or remaining in a state of inertia with business as usual, arouse their attention by turning up the heat. Emphasize the personal loss and costs associated with their current behavior using push claims and proof that is relevant to them. Create a sense of urgency by high-lighting what they have to lose—not just what the organization has to lose. Highlight the very real and personally relevant consequences of maintaining the status quo. This problem-based approach is very effective in capturing an audience's attention.

Emphasize pull if your audience is overwhelmed with pressure or in the panic zone. Highlight the benefits of your initiative and the positive outcomes for individuals, the team, and the organization. Be specific, show relevant data, and avoid broad generalizations about which of your listeners' interests will be satisfied.

Emphasize how if your audience is on board, ready to go, and already in the stretch zone. When your listeners indicate they under-stand the business case for change and are asking you how, they are in the stretch zone. Be ready with the overall plan and immediate next steps. Again, be as specific as you can be about the big steps that will have to be taken to make your vision a reality.

The Push-Pull-How Influence Strategy Builds Commitment

Once you capture the attention and interest of your target audience with a meaningful and memorable message you will need to reinforce it through follow-up. We learned that using the rational approach to influence, which engages the listener's brain—like the push-pull-how strategy discussed above and reviewed in appendix B—will create a more memorable and lasting impact. With this basic framework, you educate your audience and meet your listeners where they are today—in their thinking and in their knowledge of the subject matter.

Your influence strategy keeps the long view in mind. Knowing your audience and doing your homework in advance will prepare you for the moment, but you will want to develop a message that will endure in your listeners' hearts and minds. Since we know a cognitive approach has more enduring effects on listeners' ability to remember and repeat your message, plan to incorporate a lasting commitment to your initiative in the following manner:

- *Educate your listeners.* In building commitment for change, one of the most important tools is education. Plan to explain the rationale for changes as you teach your listeners more about the business in terms they understand and value. Help each individual understand the market, industry, and internal organizational forces that influence change. This will promote personal anticipation of and readiness for subsequent change.

- *Meet your listeners where they are.* When you introduce a new direction, system, or way of doing business, plan to meet your audience members where they are—not where you want them to be. Start by reviewing what everyone in the room already knows something about. Get people nodding their heads and speaking the same language. Only then introduce new language and new material. You may relate your information or initiative to this prior knowledge. Compare and contrast the new with the old, but always begin with a common point of reference. Your premeeting analysis will help you know what your audience already knows. If the audience members are from different organizations or walks of life, start with a simple metaphor or analogy that everyone can appreciate and understand.

- *Prepare to tell a memorable story.* Many seasoned influencers introduce their topic with a story that creates interest. The story might illustrate a current problem or dilemma from the perspective of a customer, stakeholder, or business partner—the main character. The resolution of this dilemma becomes the central theme of the discussion.

  The story tells how dire consequences will be encountered by remaining on the current path or avoided by taking an alternative path—the solution proposed by the storyteller. It engages the listeners in the reality of the current circumstances. Depending on the purpose of the discussion, the dilemma may be resolved or the urgency to address the problem magnified. The resolution leads to a call to action.

To come full circle, the discussion closes with a recalling of the opening story.

The advantage of having a single, central theme is threefold:

- The story helps make the message interesting from the start.
- If you can evoke a picture or visual in the minds of the listeners, the point will be memorable.
- The illustration both proves and clarifies the point to be made.

■ Beginning and ending a discussion with a story creates interest, enhances memory, clarifies the message, and creates an organizing structure that feels complete to both the speaker and the listeners.

CASE STUDY
Sir David Bell and the Art of the Interest-Based Business Case

Sir David Bell, chairman of the Financial Times Group and International Youth Foundation, uses the push-pull-how influence strategy as part of a story he tells around the world.[9] His purpose is to promote awareness of the global need for education, to drive corporations to his foundation for support, and to make their efforts and funding in corporate social responsibilities more meaningful. In the brief message below, notice which of the push-pull-how strategies Bell emphasizes and consider his rationale for doing so. Also note Bell's use and placement of fact and how this might appeal to a business audience. Notice the theme or image he repeats in his opening and his closing to make his story more memorable and how he has embedded personal credibility (ethos), emotional appeal (pathos), and rational logic (logos) throughout.

There are 1.3 billion young people in the world today. Half of the world population is under the age of twenty-five, and half of these are in the lowest income bracket. One hundred million people under the age of twenty-five are unemployed, and another 150 million are making between one and two dollars a day. How serious will it be if we fail to educate this population? How corrosive is it to not have any hope of receiving an education? This problem is most acute in the poorest parts of the world.

Here is my nightmare scenario: The rich are all inside the house and the poor are all outside, looking into the house. I begin to wonder, "What will happen if they can't get in? They will explode." Mexico's unemployed youth are turning to crime. The majority of people in Palestine are under twenty-five. Will there be explosions all over the world?

When businesspeople make the connection, "These very people are our future markets," they begin to engage. When you look at different companies who say education is part of their global corporate social responsibility, I say, "This is not enough. This is not something that is done on the edge. It is what companies should be doing all the time."

"What would this look like?" Bell asks as he transitions to his strategy.

It looks like companies like Nokia who are investing in teaching entrepreneurship wherever they are in the world. It means training young people in the critical trades—electricity and plumbing. It means AIDS education to reduce the impact on the grave shortage of teachers in Africa. It means sending signals via television and mobile phones about how to access education remotely. From a geopolitical perspective, the world is so interconnected by the digital technology, this can be done. It means the power of mentoring. Everyone can be a mentor. Like the founder of International Youth Foundation, Douglas Becker, says, "Every young person needs one person who is irrationally committed to their success."

We need to create partnerships with organizations that are already doing this. This means public and private collaborations. This collaboration will marry different skills and prove it is scalable. If it can happen in one place, it can happen in another. When you do a deal in another country, pay the taxes. Then, as a taxpayer, influence the government to spend those taxes on education. The role of the government of the countries in which we do business is huge. You must encourage the government and maintain a good relationship with the governments.

Bell continues his story by speaking to a higher purpose and his personal efforts in tackling youth education.

This was driven home to me in a visit to the Serengeti National Park, where I read the anthem "It is better to light a candle than to rail against the darkness." If it is dark, if there is one candle, there is light. If there is no candle, there is only darkness. My wife and I now support a clinic in Uganda with some funding. We learned how to generate money to start doing things with very simple credit schemes. We also learned that the better the health system, the lower the population. The poorer the economy, the greater the incentive to have more children because they are free labor. Children will be working instead of learning. We must encourage education—not academic education but skills that the society needs.

"We are in the midst of class warfare and race warfare," Bell says as he begins his summary.

The world's banking failures were rescued by governments at an incredible scale, paid by huge multiples of what ordinary people make, and then the same leaders who failed pay themselves huge salaries. We risk retreating back into a mind-set of "It is not our problem," and that would be a disaster. What a disaster this will be if we don't get it right. If all the rich people are living inside the house and all the poor people are living outside, looking in.

In order to capture the attention and speak the language of his business audience, Sir David Bell begins with the facts. He quickly creates a push image of people inside or outside the safety of a home, which he also closes with to round off his story. His how is composed of a variety of actions he takes and the listener can take. Notice, however, that Bell does not have a pull in his message. He has deliberately chosen urgency over attractive outcomes. Bell intends the terrifying image of being on the inside of the house surrounded by an angry mob to push us into action.

As we have learned in this chapter, the two routes to persuasion—relational and rational—and the simple push-pull-how strategy can be easily remembered and used. The challenge comes in accurately targeting the right audience and using the appropriate strategy based on the audience's dimensions of culture, tolerance of pressure, and personal self-interests.

We began this chapter by encouraging you to think of personal experiences where you influence and persuade others. As the chapter progressed, you most likely identified with both the science and the art of influence and recognized many of the people you are influencing as you mixed and matched the descriptions of the dimensions of culture. The actions, tools, and best practices suggested below are further encouragement for you to integrate this information into your daily work and personal life.

PERSONAL INFLUENCE AND PERSUASION
Actions, Tools, and Best Practices

- *Check your balance.* Assess the degree to which your current influence relationships are based on the central route to persuasion (the rational approach) and the degree to which they are based on the peripheral route to persuasion (the relational route). The science says the rational approach is more enduring. It also says the relational route requires more regular reinforcement. Is this true for you?

- *Identify your underused and overused peripheral influence cues.* Are you using your full complement of personal characteristics—your expertise, power, likability, and similarity—when influencing others? Where do you find it easier to use a visionary, inspirational, and emotional appeal? Look back at figure 2 and the descriptions of each cue to confirm you are playing to all your strengths.

- *Put the push-pull-how to use.* This simple formula requires your persuasive claims, proof, and a high-level outline of what needs to happen. Watch how you apply these three influence strategies at home, in your work, and out in your community. Do you lean toward using one or two strategies more than the others? Given the conditions under which one is more effective than another, what does this say about how you see the current circumstances? Are you influencing on automatic pilot? Are your intuitions accurate in adjusting to the demands of a multicultural audience and applying the right strategy to the situation? Look for occasions to begin to play with using the strategy or strategies you use less often.

- *Be an anthropologist.* Imagine you are on the outside looking in at an undiscovered village and want to make some observations of the people's appearance, dress, behavioral norms, values in action, and belief in rites and rituals. Now, begin to notice how others around you are using influence strategies and what response they are generating. Your organization has a culture—whether strong or weak. Are there any norms for how influence is exerted?

You may find yourself laughing out loud when you catch your-self in the act of using more push and less pull than you wanted or needed. As previously stated in the discussion of cultural intelligence, your first self-conscious attempts at influencing across cultures may feel clumsy and transparent when you wanted poise and finesse. Part of stretching—getting out of the drone zone—is the exhilaration of the pressure that comes with a new challenge. If you are not stretch-ing, you are in the drone zone. And the drone zone is a dangerous place to build a career.

In the next chapters, we will look at how to use our influence strat-egies and knowledge of our listeners to encourage collaboration and successfully manage conflict. We will also learn how our personal network of connections can help us to target the right person—the trusted advisor of the decision makers—so that we can influence results.

Four

Practicing Collaboration and Managing Conflict

Have you ever been a part of a multicultural team that is nearing the deadline of one of its major milestones? As the deadline looms closer and tensions get higher, one-on-one interactions, group meetings, and conference calls occur more frequently and the climate feels like a pressure cooker. One group of team members has headed off in their individual directions to get things done in order to make the deadline, and the air around them crackles with their loud energy and sense of purpose. Another group has occupied a conference room, and people are standing around a whiteboard as they all speak at once in their native language, conceptualizing one member's assignment; they are not feeling the anxiety of this latest deadline. Another group of individuals is quietly working in their cubicles, waiting for someone to provide some consistent direction and review how the assignments may be more systematically redistributed for greater efficiency.

Every project with large-scale deliverables has multiple interdependencies with challenging deadlines and repercussions that create mounting pressure. The potential for breakdowns in communication is increased under stress and exacerbated by different approaches to the task, and multiple dimensions of cultures. Time zone differences mean some people are meeting face to face over their afternoon tea, others are putting their children to bed while holding a BlackBerry to their ear, and still others have reluctantly slipped from their warm beds to take a business call. As the original program scope creeps larger and deliverables become due, personal and collective ability to collaborate and manage conflict is challenged and of paramount importance. This comes with the territory of doing business.

Big Picture Scan

Before you read on, answer these questions:

- Are you ever frustrated with others you perceive as not being team players?
- Do you feel you are operating under incompatible demands and lack sufficient direction, commitment, or clear leadership?
- Have you ever suppressed your feedback to someone on your team because you worried you might be culturally inappropriate or ineffective?
- Have you ever confronted someone who appeared unwilling to share his or her opinion and regretted it as soon as the words came out of your mouth for fear of unintentionally damaging the person's "face"?
- Do you love your work but hate the frustration of getting others to cooperate?
- Do you dread the prospect of having to report someone who is failing to do as he or she promised?
- Do you prefer a harmonious work climate, do all you can to avoid confrontations, and often allow your goals and grievances to go unaddressed?
- Are you always striving for compromises when teammates appear entrenched in their opposing positions?

Every organization has built-in tensions that are critical to its success in the short and long terms. Conflict will always be present wherever specialists' resources are shared across multiple projects and are tightly managed; where there is pressure to perform with aggressive deadlines to meet; where people of different professional back-grounds use different languages and approaches to problem solving; where there is a need to keep expenses down but to invest in infra-structure, research, and development of products that may or may not pay back in the future; where there is a drive to build revenue and funding but a willingness to suffer losses in unprofitable markets to have a presence.

Intentional Tensions of the Complex International Organization

In addition to these "normal" business tensions, the complex inter-national matrix organization has "intentional tensions" deliberately baked into its design. Here is a good list to start with:

- The dual-manager reporting structure increases the possibil-ity for conflicting demands, role ambiguity, and confusion of group loyalties and memberships.

- The necessity of coordinating tasks across geographic, func-tional, and business borders requires the ability to flexibly shift resources and authorities to adapt to market trends. This creates a sense of unpredictability that taxes the individual and collec-tive ability to absorb change.

- In order to build consensus, you must coordinate the input of many virtual team members and stakeholders who have an inter-est in the project's outcome. This complexity is compounded by the necessity of communicating across time zones. This churns frustration as decision making draws on and on.

- The highly diverse and unpredictable nature of so many re-gional variables affects the market—shifting tax policies, energy policies, health policies, natural disasters, national political instability, international conflict, infrastructure weakness, tech-nological capacity, wealth, and demographics—and demands the highest quality information. To analyze and make sense of

so much rich and varied information can create a large margin
for human error, do-overs, and the fear of failure.

- The mosaic of the dimensions of cultures and the inevitable
sense of cross-cultural clumsiness can often play to one's weaknesses rather than one's strengths, which adds stress.

- Change by its very nature means saying good-bye to what you
will be leaving or losing before you can make the transition to
where you are heading. With every transition comes personal
loss and the stress that accompanies change.

Together these ingredients create the perfect recipe for conflict.
Collaboration and conflict management are crucial resources for influencing across boundaries to deliver results. Knowing tensions have
been deliberately baked into the multidimensional matrix organization, you are already better equipped to anticipate tensions and prevent full-scale conflict.

Dealing with conflict means an investment of time and mental
and emotional energy. On the other hand, surfacing conflicts quickly
and resolving them to the satisfaction of everyone produces time savings, the reduction of workplace stress, and the possibility of higher
performing teams. The ability to address and resolve conflicts quickly
clears the path for vital input and valuable participation to improve
results. All the benefits of a matrix's flexible structures and adaptable resources will be sacrificed if decision making and cooperation
are stalled due to conflict. When valuable input is withheld because
of a misunderstanding, disagreements about task-related issues can
devolve into interpersonal issues, resistance, anger, resentment, and
loss of face. Momentum is lost, projects are delayed, and the essential
relationships that form the basis for future transactions are broken.

The goals of this chapter are to clarify the concepts of collaboration and conflict management and to show you how to influence
the cooperation of others using alternative collaboration and conflict
management styles.

The Science of Collaboration

There is no standard, universally accepted definition of the term "collaboration." Usually it simply means "working together."

Collaboration begins with discovering common ground. A focus on common interests builds rapport and uncovers real similarities—a critical persuasion principle. On the other hand, once you begin bargaining over what you disagree about, it is more difficult to see what you have in common. That is, the quicker you focus on differences and conflicts, the less likely it is you will get beyond differences to common interests.

Failure to collaborate in a complex setting jeopardizes the sharing of information and the achievement of results. Developing, recognizing, and rewarding both the delivery of results and the building of collaboration must be part of any measure of performance.

CASE STUDY
Reinforcing and Rewarding Achievement and Collaboration

Three large business units were joining forces and forming a single unit under one primary leader with overall accountability for the unit's profit and loss. The strategy was to share customer information and sales goals and to reduce the costs of functional, operational, and business resources required to serve global customers. The three core product lines were once thriving independent lines of business with a history of internal competition for attracting top talent and revenue generation. The three leaders had always allowed this somewhat friendly rivalry to persist and believed it motivated individual unit innovation, excellence, and outstanding performance.

However, internal competition was no longer considered healthy or tolerated by their group executive, who appointed a single new leader for the newly integrated business. Now the three once-independent business leaders were one layer removed from the group executive. The three leaders were told by the group executive himself that collaboration would be the key to building a sustainable and competitive business and were given one set of common goals: reduce and share the costs of technology solutions and operations, streamline product and service offerings, improve the customer experience, increase the revenue of shared customers, and prioritize and share the right information for the best decision making. A temporary executive leadership transition committee was designed specifically for this integration and included the three original business leaders and the regionally assigned chiefs of sales, technology, risk, services, and operations.

This international three-business integration was launched following months of speculation and planning by the executive committee with a conference of the top fifty managers. These managers represented the multiple matrix dimensions: customer segment, product, regions, and functions. The group executive expressed his sense of urgency, support, and expectations—as did the new leader of the integrated business unit and each of the product heads. The mission, goals, roles, and initial structures and procedures were all presented. Challenges were discussed. Immediate and near-term actions were outlined. Project and program owners were introduced.

A change management communication strategy was developed for the next eighteen months with a calendar of quarterly face-to-face meetings to be held around the world, rotating into each region. In a climate of severe cost containment and restricted travel allowances, the leadership team felt this investment in face-to-face communication sent a strong signal of their commitment to this union.

In order to emphasize the critical importance of moving from a competitive to a collaborative mind-set, the three original business leaders proposed to the executive committee that they establish common, high-reaching performance goals. They would reward the top fifty senior managers' collective achievement of those goals and their ability to collaborate. The executive committee gave their support and agreed to attach a percentage of the top fifty senior managers' annual bonus to their ability to collaborate. Ten percent of their annual bonus was attached to measured improvement in collaboration behaviors and would be awarded on an all-or-nothing basis. This was the first time in the history of the organization that a monetary reward would be attached to anything other than a performance goal. The senior managers' ability to collaborate would be rated by themselves, their various dotted- and solid-line managers, and nine of their peers from around the world who influenced the delivery of results and who were approved by their dotted- and solid-line managers.

The participating senior managers were introduced to the Peer Collaboration Valued Behavior Rating Scale.[1] The on-line survey defined collaboration in five target value categories: focus on collective results, commit to decisions, exercise accountability, develop trust, and engage in constructive conflict. Each of the five value categories was illustrated with twelve representative behaviors. A brief introduction to the five categories was presented to ensure the group held a common understanding of what collaboration looked like. Following this introduction, a baseline measure for each senior manager was taken, including a self-, peer, and management assessment. A follow-up date was set in nine months to readminister the self-peer-manager rating before bonuses would be awarded.

The baseline results pointed to the need for improvement in five behaviors most frequently mentioned across the fifty senior managers:

- Pay attention to what is happening outside their part of the work (focus on collective results).

- Set clear standards for themselves and others and make those standards explicit (exercise accountability).

- Call others on their failure to meet established standards of performance or behavior (exercise accountability).

- Move toward conflict, not away from it (engage in constructive conflict).

- Begin with neutrality rather than judgment or condemnation (engage in constructive conflict).

Each individual received his or her personal results in a private coaching session. Group results were distributed and discussed during the next quarterly senior management off-site, where recurring themes were presented for discussion and training delivered on collaboration and conflict management. On-line resources and tool kits illustrating and reinforcing best practices were distributed. Regional coaches were trained and appointed to provide ongoing individual and team support.

All in all, the leaders of this integrated new business put in place several practical support mechanisms to manage the change to this new culture of collaboration: a leadership mandate, governance structure, and clear P&L accountability; goal alignment and incentive reinforcement; group communication vehicles and platforms; and individual and group development support.

Anticipating and Identifying Systemic Barriers to Collaboration

Despite this holistic attempt to manage the change toward an integrated business, success was complicated by three systemic failures: failure to address and blend the three diverse business cultures; failure to acknowledge and manage around entrenched, incompatible technology systems, applications, and analytics; and failure to maintain continuity of vision with midcourse changes of leadership. For example, each of the original business cultures approached customers in a different way. One line of business was more transactional and depended on sophisticated analytics for data-driven decision making. Another business was more customer-relationship oriented with a deep sales force dedicated to its prime customers—but using what the first business considered sloppy or nonexistent analytics in its decision making. The third business believed that the term "sales" was vulgar and should not appear anywhere in its discussions, documentation, or approach to customers. It was based on high-end customers that deserved high-touch customer relationships focused on a vast range of product features and functions tailored to the unique needs of each customer.

In addition to cultural differences, the customer-facing and back-room operations solutions were heavily dependent on technology. The technology infrastructures in each region were not only unique but still in development and unique to each product. Standardizing the architecture while conducting business requires vast technology investment and patience—and both investment dollars and patience can be in short supply, particularly in short-term-oriented business cultures. The ambitious ongoing technology planning and cumbersome delivery hindered the creation of a single version of the truth regarding the customers and the company's finances.

In addition, the leadership changed within six months of the launch of the integration. Two of the three original business leaders were assigned to other international assignments, and the executive appointed as their leader was given the additional assignment as acting chief of international compliance.

These organizational systemic and cultural barriers were compounded by the global financial crisis and stringent regulatory oversight. These results-driven managers were bombarded with challenges to achieve their goals. The valued behaviors of collaboration were well communicated, understood, and beginning to be applied. By the end of the year, managers' peer collaboration scores improved, but the original vision, leadership, and sense of possibilities were overtaken by cynicism and the fear of job loss.

Peer Collaboration Behaviors

Five key values show up in the research on collaboration and were used in the above case: focus on collective results, commit to decisions, exercise accountability, develop trust, and engage in constructive conflict. The following sections provide descriptions of these values, which you will find useful to compare and contrast with your teams' behaviors.

Focus on Collective Results

When people focus on collective results, they give top priority to the good of the whole rather than individual results, including their own. They contribute to establishing targets for the collective results and pay attention to what is happening outside their own part of the work. They ask for the help and resources they need to achieve results and offer their resources, time, and expertise as needed for a task. They ask for no more than their fair share of the available resources. They also ask for the help they need to meet requirements, and they accept being rewarded and compensated based on the results of the whole rather than just their own part. They fairly balance their own interests with those of others and the whole.

Commit to Decisions

People express their commitment to decisions when they clearly and openly share their own views before the decisions are made. They take the opportunity to hear others' views and rationales for other options and believe their own views have been heard. A commitment to decisions requires people to recognize that decisions must often be made without perfect information and still consider the decision-making process fair. People do not insist that all decisions be made by consensus. Once a decision is made, they agree to take it as their own, even if it is not their personal preference or choice. They do not continue to complain about the decision or ask to revisit it. They behave as if the decision were their number one choice and do everything in their power to deliver the results the decision entails.

Exercise Accountability

People tend to exercise accountability effectively when they set clear standards for themselves and others and make those standards explicit. They aim high, rather than playing it safe with unchallenging goals, and do what they commit to and are accountable for. They regularly monitor their performance and that of others for progress in meeting goals and standards. People take responsibility for what they do or do not do and the consequences of their actions or inaction. Exercising accountability means they do not make excuses. When members of the team fail to meet established standards of performance or behavior, they address it. And they really listen to and take in feedback from others on their own performance. They call attention to any gradual weakening or disregard of the standards.

Develop Trust

People tend to develop trust in relationships when they do what they say they will—they are consistent and competent—and say what they cannot do. They tell the truth, saying honestly what they think, feel, and see. They avoid needlessly hurting others. They forgive a fair amount and listen. They are willing to honestly express uncertainty, doubt, confusion, or other vulnerabilities. They take the risk of putting themselves in another's hands. They act with integrity and they are honest with themselves.

Engage in Constructive Conflict

People tend to manage conflict effectively when they move toward a conflict, not away from it. They surface the conflict with the person they have a difference with, not bystanders or other parties. They are willing and able to bear whatever anxiety confronting the conflict entails. They respect the other person in their difference and separate the person from the issue. They ask, rather than infer, the motivations or intentions of the person they are in conflict with. They are aware of their personal biases and perceptions and hold them up for scrutiny by themselves and their teams. People who are able to engage in constructive feedback begin with neutrality, rather than judgment or condemnation. Despite anxiety, they do not hold back their contrary views because they are afraid they will be hurt if they express them. They state their views clearly without filtering them and make their differences with the other person explicit.

Scan Your Team's Collaboration Behaviors

Now that you understand the behaviors needed for effective collaboration, take a look at your team or organization. Rate your team members on each of the following items on a scale of 1 to 5, where 1 means "seldom" and 5 means "usually."

Focus on Collective Results

___ Contribute to establishing targets for collective results.

___ Give top priority to collective rather than individual results.

___ Pay attention to what is happening outside their part of the work.

___ Ask for no more than their fair share of available resources.

___ Make every effort to make others look good.

Commit to Decisions

___ Clearly and openly express their own views before a decision is made.

___ Do not continue to ask to revisit the decision once it has been made.

___ Publicly and privately support the decision enthusiastically and convey agreement on messages about the decision.

___ Do everything in their power to deliver the results of the decision.

Exercise Accountability

___ Set clear standards for themselves and others and make those standards explicit.

___ Call themselves and others on their failure to meet established standards of performance or behavior.

___ Really listen to and take in feedback from others on their own performance.

___ Call attention to any gradual weakening or disregard for standards.

Develop Trust

___ Do what they say they will do—competently.

___ Listen.

___ Honestly express uncertainty, doubt, confusion, or other vulnerabilities.

___ Say what they cannot do.

___ Take the risk of putting themselves in another's hands.

Engage in Constructive Conflict
___ Move toward conflict, not away from it.
___ Begin with neutrality, rather than judgment or condemnation.
___ State their views clearly without filtering them, and make their differences with the other person plain and unambiguous.
___ Surface the conflict with the person they have a difference with, not bystanders or other parties.

These behaviors set a very high bar and are challenging for individuals from all dimensions of culture—some clearly more than others, as we will see in a moment. Out of the twenty-two statements, how many describe your team or the culture of your organization as a whole? If you go back and rate *yourself*, how would you rate?

Before reading further, reflect for a moment on the behaviors you would like to see more of in your team or organization.

Cultural Dimensions in Practicing Collaboration and Managing Conflict

As you read through the list of behaviors above, you probably noticed how many of the behaviors appear within the dimension of culture described in figure 1 (chapter 2). Assertiveness and cooperativeness are essential to collaboration. However, assertiveness in one culture may be perceived as aggression in another. Research across cultures shows this to be particularly true regarding stereotypes about women in business.[2]

Although conflict is routinely avoided in organizations, the behaviors in this scan demonstrate a bias for confronting rather than avoiding conflict. This assumes that participating in a discussion where there is disagreement will provide the opportunity to express diverse views in order to come to a meeting of the minds and resolution. This open communication style may fit with members of cultures that value accuracy, strive to avoid ambiguity, and are familiar with frank and open communication. Cultures that value diplomacy and tolerate ambiguity will expect disagreements to be aired privately.

CASE STUDY
Practicing Collaboration and Managing Conflict as a Team

Brian Lupinski is distressed about the breakdown in communication among his team members and the likelihood they will fail to make their first important task deadline today—confirming his doubts about their ability to collaborate.

This is Brian's first internationally based team with managers reporting to him and their local regional managers in China, India, and Brazil. His predecessor required that team members direct all their communication to himself, so team members rarely spoke to one another. Brian's style is very different. Already he has instituted regular team meetings via conference calls. His new manager told him she valued face-to-face meetings. Brian has already visited each of his new regional managers in their home offices and has budgeted for one such face-to-face meeting a year. He has a video-cam on his laptop and has required the same of each of his regional managers so they can see one another as they confer.

Brian has noticed the different styles of communication in each of his regional managers and he does not know yet how much of these he might attribute to personality or to culture. For example, in the past, he had been accustomed to lively and candid team discussions of issues of importance. At the conclusion of these discussions, he would rarely have to ask before someone would volunteer to take responsibility for following up on, addressing, and reporting back to the group on the issue. Now he feels he has to call on each team member to express his or her view in turn.

Almost immediately after he took his new position, the deadline for the year's budget was announced. Brian and his team had a simple task that required the team to collaborate. After their first budget discussion, Brian asked for a volunteer to follow up on an action item and report back at the next meeting. His request was met with silence. He rephrased his request in case he was unclear. He still had no takers. Finally, he asked that each of his managers think about the topic and get back to him by the end of that day to lead the task. But by the end of the next day, he still had no volunteers, and Brian saw one more day in this very short budget time frame tick by.

Brian asked his manager for advice. "Do not ask for volunteers again," she said. "Make the assignment. Be specific in your expectations." Disappointed in this top-down, hierarchical approach, Brian complied nonetheless. He believed that if his regional managers were going to be accountable down the road, they would have to build commitment among their teams to important decisions about next year's budget by clearly and openly expressing their views now.

Three weeks later and just days away from the budget deadline, Brian complained that each of his regional managers was asking for much more than was reasonable or a fair share: "If we are to focus on our collective results—our project as a whole, not just each of the regions separately—we cannot have this old-school mentality of budget padding or sandbagging" (i.e., deliberately asking for more than is needed as a negotiation tactic).

On the day of the deadline, Brian completed a long phone call with his on-site team leader in India. Rizwan still retained two very different versions of his budget: the original wish list he had submitted three weeks before and the latest revised, more realistic, and closest-to-final version he and Brian had discussed just last week. One hour before their call, Rizwan had submitted his original highly inflated budget with no accompanying message. It took another hour's debate before Brian could persuade Rizwan to send the revised budget. Brian feared this same conversation would be repeated with his other two managers and had little faith that Rizwan would submit an appropriate budget. In order to meet global finance's deadline, Brian would have to skip the conversation he had planned with his entire team so he could rationalize their budgets into a single document. He hung his head in despair. He was failing miserably and it would be apparent to his peers up the line.

Which Cultural Dimensions May Be Turning into Team Conflict?

As you read Brian's story, what cultural dimensions did you see that may be turning into team conflict? For example, time may be a dilemma here. Look at the dimensions associated with time in figure 6. Rizwan is from a culture (India) where people are less focused on deadlines and sequences of events and more aware of many activities, work requirements, projects, and interests going on at once. Figure 6 describes the possible cross-cultural misunderstandings that may lead to conflict.

What Collaboration Behaviors Might Brian Want to Reinforce among His Team Members?

Brian began to make the connection between cultural differences, the rising tension within his team, and the failure of the team to collaborate. Until Brian can find a way to reconcile these dilemmas, he and his team members will continue to misunderstand each other and tensions will rise.

For example, Brian believes that focusing on collective results is the cornerstone to collaboration. He also believes that his team members will be more committed to decisions if they have a say in what those decisions are—particularly when it comes to the budget. His manager insisted on a top-down approach, while Brian wants his team to buy into the budget by openly expressing their opinions at the beginning of the process.

In the following discussion, the dilemmas or questions raised in this budget-building example are described and some advice is provided to Brian to reconcile the differences.

- *Dilemma 1—Significance of power and status:* Brian is egalitarian and his team is hierarchical. Brian wants to consult with his team for better buy-in. The team members want to please Brian and want him to take charge and tell them what to do.

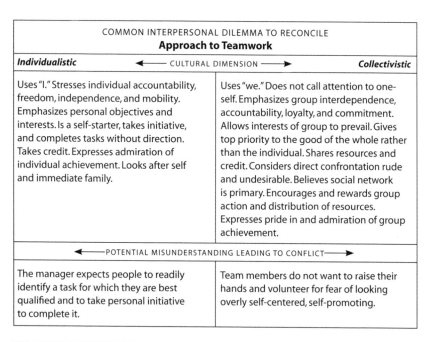

COMMON INTERPERSONAL DILEMMA TO RECONCILE	
Approach to Teamwork	
Individualistic ◄— CULTURAL DIMENSION —►	*Collectivistic*
Uses "I." Stresses individual accountability, freedom, independence, and mobility. Emphasizes personal objectives and interests. Is a self-starter, takes initiative, and completes tasks without direction. Takes credit. Expresses admiration of individual achievement. Looks after self and immediate family.	Uses "we." Does not call attention to oneself. Emphasizes group interdependence, accountability, loyalty, and commitment. Allows interests of group to prevail. Gives top priority to the good of the whole rather than the individual. Shares resources and credit. Considers direct confrontation rude and undesirable. Believes social network is primary. Encourages and rewards group action and distribution of resources. Expresses pride in and admiration of group achievement.
◄—POTENTIAL MISUNDERSTANDING LEADING TO CONFLICT—►	
The manager expects people to readily identify a task for which they are best qualified and to take personal initiative to complete it.	Team members do not want to raise their hands and volunteer for fear of looking overly self-centered, self-promoting.

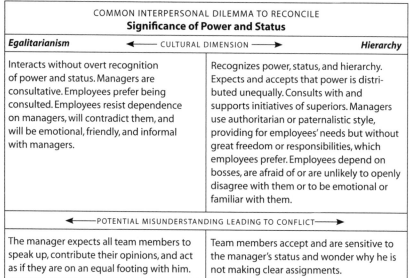

COMMON INTERPERSONAL DILEMMA TO RECONCILE	
Significance of Power and Status	
Egalitarianism ◄— CULTURAL DIMENSION —►	*Hierarchy*
Interacts without overt recognition of power and status. Managers are consultative. Employees prefer being consulted. Employees resist dependence on managers, will contradict them, and will be emotional, friendly, and informal with managers.	Recognizes power, status, and hierarchy. Expects and accepts that power is distributed unequally. Consults with and supports initiatives of superiors. Managers use authoritarian or paternalistic style, providing for employees' needs but without great freedom or responsibilities, which employees prefer. Employees depend on bosses, are afraid of or are unlikely to openly disagree with them or to be emotional or familiar with them.
◄—POTENTIAL MISUNDERSTANDING LEADING TO CONFLICT—►	
The manager expects all team members to speak up, contribute their opinions, and act as if they are on an equal footing with him.	Team members accept and are sensitive to the manager's status and wonder why he is not making clear assignments.

Figure 6 Dimensions of culture contributing to misunderstandings and potential conflict

COMMON INTERPERSONAL DILEMMA TO RECONCILE **Importance of Task versus Relationship**	
Performance and task oriented (low context) ← CULTURAL DIMENSION →	*Cooperation and relationship oriented (high context)*
Is direct. Asserts opinion. Appears stern. Believes in importance of transactions, tasks, and facts first. May appear loud and interrupts others. Appears self-assured and may appear arrogant. Appears to act regardless of cues in the setting, i.e., low context or situational awareness. Is competitive. Strives to win. Creates opportunities for personal advancement, higher earnings, and recognition. Accepts conflict and confrontation.	Is indirect. Listens for cues in the setting about how to adapt tone and behavior, i.e., high context. Emphasizes relationship first, transaction later. Desires to please. Strives to have good relationship with direct superior, cooperative relationships with coworkers, and high quality of life. Strives for win-win solution. Resists standing out. Is modest.
←——POTENTIAL MISUNDERSTANDING LEADING TO CONFLICT——→	
The manager expects a direct and forthright expression of concerns and issues. He is confused that team members do not see this as an opportunity to step forward and shine.	Team members feel they are giving the manager what he is asking for and have a high desire to please. Team members are working on establishing a relationship with the manager. Team members are not accustomed to analyzing and critiquing a manager's work.

COMMON INTERPERSONAL DILEMMA TO RECONCILE **Communication**	
Accuracy, uncertainty avoidance ← CULTURAL DIMENSION →	*Diplomacy, ambiguity tolerance*
Highly values explicit truth and accuracy. Feels the threat of the unknown. Prefers predictability. Prefers rules--written and unwritten. Openly discusses people, events, things, and inner feelings. Overtly strives for accuracy and precision in communication.	Believes everything is relative. Says, "It depends." Desires harmony in communication and relationships. Is sensitive to the feelings and reputations of others. Gives and expects to receive bad news in private. Is open to innovation and uncertainty.

Communication continues on next page

Figure 6 (continued)

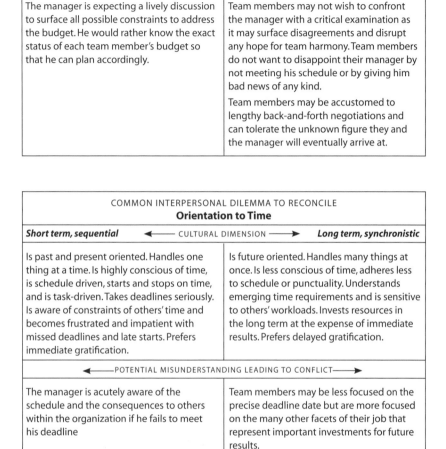

Communication	
◄——— POTENTIAL MISUNDERSTANDING LEADING TO CONFLICT ———►	
The manager is expecting a lively discussion to surface all possible constraints to address the budget. He would rather know the exact status of each team member's budget so that he can plan accordingly.	Team members may not wish to confront the manager with a critical examination as it may surface disagreements and disrupt any hope for team harmony. Team members do not want to disappoint their manager by not meeting his schedule or by giving him bad news of any kind.
	Team members may be accustomed to lengthy back-and-forth negotiations and can tolerate the unknown figure they and the manager will eventually arrive at.

COMMON INTERPERSONAL DILEMMA TO RECONCILE **Orientation to Time**	
Short term, sequential ◄——— CULTURAL DIMENSION ———► *Long term, synchronistic*	
Is past and present oriented. Handles one thing at a time. Is highly conscious of time, is schedule driven, starts and stops on time, and is task-driven. Takes deadlines seriously. Is aware of constraints of others' time and becomes frustrated and impatient with missed deadlines and late starts. Prefers immediate gratification.	Is future oriented. Handles many things at once. Is less conscious of time, adheres less to schedule or punctuality. Understands emerging time requirements and is sensitive to others' workloads. Invests resources in the long term at the expense of immediate results. Prefers delayed gratification.
◄——— POTENTIAL MISUNDERSTANDING LEADING TO CONFLICT ———►	
The manager is acutely aware of the schedule and the consequences to others within the organization if he fails to meet his deadline	Team members may be less focused on the precise deadline date but are more focused on the many other facets of their job that represent important investments for future results.

Figure 6 (continued)

Advice: Brian needs to emphasize how happy it will make him to receive his team members' ideas and appeal to their desire to please their superior.

- *Dilemma 2—Teamwork:* Brian is individualistic and expects individual team members to take independent initiative. The team members are largely collectivistic, prefer to act as a group for the good of the group rather than individually, and resist calling attention to themselves.

  Advice: Brian can appeal to the team members' value of cooperation and interdependence by emphasizing how each individual's input is only the first step of a collaborative process critical to the result of the whole. He might emphasize how the team will be rewarded by him for their collective efforts in working together to solve this important problem.

- *Dilemma 3—Importance of task versus relationship:* Brian wants his team to commit to decisions and believes this is best achieved by having everyone provide input. Brian is task oriented and his team is relationship oriented. He wants the team members to assert their opinions and offer facts. The team members want to get to know each other and Brian before trusting the group with their input and risking losing face.

  Advice: Brian could take time to schedule a one-on-one call with each of his team members prior to any future decision to explain the problem or opportunity and solicit individual opinions—very similar to the Japanese *nemawashi* practice of reaching consensus. Whereas that process does not include a large group discussion of possible solutions, Brian could gradually progress to his ideal of open group brainstorming and collaborative decision making.

Brian was very clear about his expectations for the kind of budget information he needed and by when. Rizwan delayed his submission and failed to submit the correct information. Brian initially gave Rizwan the benefit of the doubt and wrote this off to differences in time orientation.

Another international manager Brian often turns to for advice, Sue Leung, believes you have to confront someone who may be holding out and unwilling to make any concessions. "This is competitive behavior that has no place in this collaborative exercise," Sue said. "This guy is not playing with the team." She told Brian she had someone like this on her team. She quickly pulled him to the side and told him he would have to straighten out or get off the team. He straightened out and stayed on the team and did his job. Before Brian takes Sue's advice, however, he will want to continue to put tasks before the team to complete and develop as a team. He will need to remember that his predecessor never coached the team, only individual players, and a team isn't built overnight.

What's fascinating about Brian's team is the fact that they agree on the most important value: they all want to collaborate. They all want to focus on collective results. However, their culturally hard-wired assumptions about how to be a team and the role of leaders are different. These are not insignificant differences and could lead to conflict. But rather than manage the conflict, Brian should create his influence steppingstone strategy toward the goal of getting the group to focus on managing agreement. First and foremost in his influence strategy, he will have to build trust and relationships as the foundation for future high team performance.

Now that we have explored how to address cultural differences that can lead to breakdowns in communication, teamwork, and collaboration, the next section describes some alternative styles of managing conflict that you are likely to use and encounter as you cross cultural boundaries to deliver results. Being armed with the knowledge of a range of styles or approaches to managing conflict will help you apply your cultural intelligence.

Balancing Self-Interests and Other Interests

In our discussions of culture, we described one potential dilemma related to teamwork. Members of one end of this spectrum of dimensions are "collectivistic," and they distinguish themselves as being other oriented, emphasizing team members' dependence on one another, team loyalty, and sharing of credit among team members. The interests of the group supersede personal interests. At the other end, members are more self-oriented or "individualistic."

Research in collaboration and conflict management shows a similar spirit. The familiar term "win-win" (collaboration) is consistent with the collectivistic dimension and "win-lose" (competition) is consistent with the individualistic dimension. The cultural orientation to either compete or collaborate can be so profoundly stitched into the pattern of one's behavior that an alternative approach seems foreign, it requires a totally different mind-set, and the behavior has to be learned.

We also discussed the cultural dimensions related to one's orientation to time. Some cultures are more now oriented and desire the immediate gratification of needs and interests. Other cultures are more future oriented, tolerate delayed gratification, and look to the long-term payoffs of current investments at the expense of immediate results. These now or later orientations to time create different perceptions of pressure and urgency. Win now and get results now, or be patient because this investment of effort and resources will pay off at some time in the future.

Following an introduction to cultural dimensions and the potential for friction, a recently promoted international manager was asked by his solid-line manager to choose one of these dimensions to describe himself. He quickly chose the individualistic dimension. She then asked him to choose one dimension to describe the organization's cultural DNA. He quickly chose the collectivistic dimension. She finally asked him what the difference between his cultural dimension and the organization's cultural dimension might mean for him. "What's it going to be like to be an 'I' person in a 'we' culture, you mean?" He said he never realized how his success thus far had depended on his ability to compete or that the organization was clearly one that valued collaboration. He also said he wondered if he could make the shift. What about the whole concept of playing to his strengths? His new manager told him this was a good question to reflect on and that she would continue to check with him throughout his first six months in this new job.

The following example shows someone who struggles to shift her mind-set from competition to collaboration and who will benefit from coaching from a trusted colleague as she makes the shift.

CASE STUDY
Jo Marquez Shifts from a Competitive to a Collaborative Mind-Set

Jo Marquez is a successful retailer who serves on the regional board of an international nonprofit organization's spay-and-neuter program to control the number of unwanted puppies and kittens throughout her region. She is a passionate animal advocate and devotes considerable free time to the development of funding for this nonprofit. She recently learned that a similar organization is preparing to launch an ambitious funding campaign in a territory that overlaps her region. Jo's funding was severely reduced due to the economic recession and she was furious about the idea of another group encroaching on and competing within her region for the same, limited funds. The board members of the other organization have invited Jo and her team to join them in a meeting to discuss development issues. Jo and her team began preparing a defensive and competitive strategy to persuade this other organization to leave her region.

Jo confided to her professional network in earlier conversations that her organization did not have the kind of mailing lists and technology infrastructure of her competitor. She knew she would have to move way out of her comfort zone and the current funding constraints to compete technologically. One of her networking peers, Ana, suggested this problem sounded like it needed more than a win-lose competitive battle. Competition is great, she said, when you have to protect your interests when you are under attack. But these two groups had a common love and concern for animal welfare, and this overarching common goal was the right situation for collaboration. There may be another solution that will meet both groups' needs, and they could end up friends rather than adversaries in the end.

Never in any of Jo's thinking or her discussions with her board members or her professional network did the idea of joining forces or collaborating with this other organization come to mind. It took several rounds of discussions with Ana for Jo to even understand what her organization might gain from collaborating or what collaboration might look like.

Jo's business success had come from competing, so what could possibly compel her to consider developing an influence strategy to cooperate? The process of uncovering mutual goals and leveraging each other's strengths and organizational resources not only felt foreign to her, it felt drawn out and complex. Ana conceded this point— it could take longer. And the other group may try to exploit Jo's group. Jo felt much more comfortable with her board's original plan to compete and win. This would immediately put her organization back on the familiar ground of doing business independently.

So deeply rooted is Jo's cultural DNA to compete, the idea of collaborating was literally incomprehensible. Being familiar with immediate, short-term wins, Jo could not fathom the idea of investing time and energy in developing a new working relationship with a "competitor." She could not imagine the benefit of delay. From a persuasion and influence perspective, a rational approach—getting Jo to think about the relevance of this new approach—would be premature. The only reason she listened to Ana was that she knew Ana, liked her, and believed Ana was an expert in this area (all personal characteristics, all peripheral or relational influences). Jo voluntarily declared her commitment to the goal of considering a collaborative approach in front of her entire professional networking group— another peripheral influence strategy (consistency—voluntarily and publicly declaring one's intention strengthens one's resolve to follow through). Finally, we know from chapter 3 that peripheral influence does not last as long as central or rational influence, and Ana committed to calling Jo on a weekly basis to discuss her latest thinking. Jo's goal became Ana's goal, and Ana's influence goal is to coach Jo through her first attempt at collaboration.

Jo Marquez's example illustrates just how conditioned we can be to move into one conflict management mode without considering alternatives. Her story also reinforces the value of having a mentor or supporter when trying out any new resource for the first time.

The Impact of Task versus Relationship Orientation on Managing Conflict

Another dimension of culture that affects managing conflict is the degree to which people pay attention to the situation or context in which a relationship or transaction takes place—low context or high context. Members of low-context cultures tend to be direct, assertive, task oriented, and competitive—more win-lose as a default setting like Jo in the previous example. Members of high-context cultures take their cues from the situation or context and tend to be more indirect, cooperative, and relationship oriented—more win-win as a default setting. This idea of taking cues from the setting allows for a situation-by-situation or "it depends" approach to managing conflict effectively.

This tolerance for ambiguity also differentiates people's communication styles. Members of some cultures desire harmony in relationships and will avoid sharing bad news or disconfirming feedback in any public manner. If there is bad news or negative feedback to be shared, if it is shared at all, it will be shared in private to protect the "face" of the other person. If there is a dispute about direction, members of these cultures are more likely to accommodate the will of others. On the other hand, members of cultures that do not tolerate ambiguity will strive to create certainty and predictability through the use of rules and statements of fact. Harmony and face will be put aside to get to truth, accuracy, and facts through open discussion—even if that includes giving critical feedback about a project or a person in the room.

Taking these dimensions of culture into consideration, people will manage conflict in a number of ways, as shown in figure 7:

- From a self-only orientation, with no or low consideration of the other or of an ongoing relationship, the default mode will be to compete—and to compete to win. It's win-lose: I win, you lose. This assertive stance is absolutely appropriate when you must protect your self-interests or make sure you are being heard. On the other hand, the potential damage to relationships is high.

- From an other-only orientation, with no or low consideration of one's self-interests for the sake of harmony, to support others in need, or to do a favor for someone, the default mode will be to accommodate the other's desires. It's still win-lose, but this time I lose; you win. Each of us will be persuaded by someone else and will naturally concede.

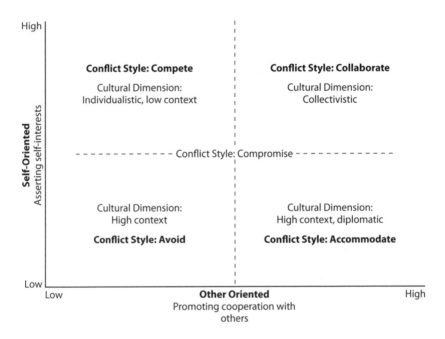

Figure 7 Alternative conflict management styles and dimensions of culture[3]

- From a meeting-in-the-middle perspective—I get some of my self-interests met and you get some of your self-interests met—compromising is in order. This is another form of win-lose: I win a little and lose a little; you win a little and lose a little. When all efforts to collaborate or compete and win have failed, this is the most practical conflict management mode.

- From an orientation of meeting personal self interests and meeting the other's self-interests, this is collaboration. It's a win-win proposition where you win all you want and I win all I want, too.

- From the point of view of complete dismissal of either's interest, the option taken is to avoid the conflict of interests altogether. In this case, I walk away from the engagement without getting what I want, and you walk away from the engagement without getting what you want.

In an international setting it is very likely you will have all of these mind-sets and assumptions running on autopilot during any disagreement. Brian's steppingstone influence strategy to bring his group of individuals along in their ability to collaborate as a high performing team is a useful image to keep in mind.

In Jo's example, we saw how she was hard-wired to compete. To persuade Jo to move away from one approach to managing conflict to another approach required her peer, Ana, to plan an influence strategy. Jo could not understand central, rational evidence of why another conflict management strategy might work better than her default approach, so Ana led with a relational or peripheral influence strategy.

From a personal perspective, you can appreciate that different situations and different cultural orientations require different conflict management styles just as they do different influence strategies. Members of some cultures—like your own—may have a firmly patterned response to views that are incompatible with their own views. So a good place to start is to recognize if you use one mode of conflict management most often. Are you most likely to compete, collaborate, compromise, avoid, or accommodate? Then ask yourself when you are most flexible moving from one style to another. What cues in the setting or context do you pick up on your cultural intelligence radar to indicate when one style might be more effective than another? Knowing your cultural dimensions, personal values, practices, strengths, and weaknesses when it comes to managing conflict is essential.

From an organizational perspective, the complex, multidimensional matrix organization has intentional tensions baked into its structure that make conflicts inevitable and desirable. Top management's responsibility is to also bake into the organizational structure mechanisms that surface information compatible and incompatible with common or popular views, establish a forum for discussing and debating views, and establish a decision-making process that takes alternative and seemingly incompatible views into account.

CASE STUDY
Sue Leung Stretches Her Ability to Manage Conflict

Sue Leung's areas of responsibility are growing by leaps and bounds. As a result, she has been able to add people from around the world to her team. "When I'm looking to fill a job," Sue said, "the first question I ask people is, 'Where have you delivered real value to the organization?'" Once their ability to perform has been established, she asks them to describe *how* they deliver results. If their method isn't obvious in their answer, Sue always gets to the question of how they get people to collaborate and how they handle resistance. "How do you sell your ideas to others? Have you played a team sport? Do you push back?"

"Now confrontation I'm less good at," Sue admitted. "I used to be very good at listening and weighing all the angles and coming to consensus. But the truth is, you have to be able to push for one thing up front." Sue's initiative included the development of new products and services in emerging markets. The organization's historical success had been dependent on the handful of products it had developed decades ago. Promoting, selling, and servicing these tried-and-true products on-line highlighted just how few products and services were available for the unique Southern Asia and Latin American markets. Sue's team needed to build a framework to move quickly in new product development, but she faced resistance in launching her idea.

"I presented such a framework to our business group. And these people said, 'Who's going to approve this?' They hemmed and hawed and had all kinds of objections and asked who would need to approve this and that. I just said, 'I'm asking you to vet this. Put it through your own careful examination to ensure its suitability. Where you find holes, I'm asking you to inform me and give me your input. But I'm going to publish this framework with or without you.'

"They all settled down and promised to give me input. I got an e-mail from one of the guys on the team that evening that said, 'Steady now, Sue.' Apparently, I had raised my voice on the phone and everyone on the videoconference could see me rise from my chair and point. Everyone did come back with input and feedback. There was nothing they could add and the work got done."

Sue faced the resistance of her entire team, and she switched into competition as a conflict management mode. She needed to assert her opinion because she knew from experience that she was right. Her team was pushing back, so she had to assert her authority and push through. She expressed her self-doubt when she related this example, saying "I'm not good at confrontation." This self-doubt could be born of lack of experience. The more she asserts her opinion, the more comfortable she will become, particularly as she gets good coaching and feedback. The "Steady now, Sue" comment from her male colleague would not fall into the category of good coaching and feedback and may have contributed to her second-guessing her finesse. Sue will have to keep in mind that across the globe, women are more likely than men to be considered inappropriately aggressive when they are being assertive.[4] Tensions and resistance can come from many sources, two of which are the subject of this book: cultural differences and the structural tensions the international matrix organization structure produces.

MANAGING INTENTIONAL TENSIONS
What Can Top Management Do?

Sharing resources across functions and businesses provides optimum flexibility to adjust to changes in the marketplace. It means the power inherent in temporarily "owning" these rich resources will shift regularly. Power imbalances are frequent in the matrix organization and are tensions that are intentionally built into the structure to maintain flexibility and responsiveness to the market.

Top management's responsibility is to create some reasonable semblance of a balance of power. Power can be recalibrated by using pay, job titles, access to the most senior managers, or reporting level within a hierarchy.[5]

The structural complexity of the international matrix or shared services organization requires extreme coordination and is another predictable tension that can produce conflict. Work is spread among multiple initiatives, programs, and project teams with overlapping interests of a variety of sponsors, sources of funds, and stakeholders.

Whether the regions, products, and functions within a global organization are loosely coupled or tightly linked, when an organization's products or services depend on the cooperative efforts of a variety of specialists from multiple functional units, a different kind of managerial behavior is required than that of conventionally structured single-line-of-authority organizations.

We have said earlier that cooperation, sharing of resources, management control, and collaboration require a culture that encourages open management of conflict. Wherever an imbalance of power exists—one function is temporarily critical for success or one line of business is requiring a special infusion of human capital—a way of understanding this redistribution of power must be created.

The key to success in a complex matrix environment is a culture in which top leaders anticipate the tensions that are intentionally built into the structure. From the top of the organization, this would mean to formally create the expectation among leaders to anticipate and identify potential areas of competition and conflict. Top managers can create a forum that legitimizes and encourages debate. Heads of executive committees can expect these meetings to establish a process for surfacing and resolving differences using ground rules that include some decision-making methodology. This is more than the standard project prioritization, with decision criteria that are vetted and accepted. The person or persons at the top must make it widely known that they expect creative tension, conflict, and heated debate from leaders of business lines and functions. Having a process in place helps model and ensure that a wide variety of perspectives receive attention and debate.

Decisions do not always require full agreement or consensus. The person or persons at the top theoretically are ultimately responsible. However, given all the stakeholders and wide distribution of shared roles and responsibilities, reaching at least a critical mass of support is essential because what follows is execution, which requires collaboration.

CASE STUDY
Sally Woo's Trust Tensions with Finance and IT

The notoriety of Sally Woo's large finance project in Canada attracted high expectations for her next project in Malaysia. She and her IT team were given no leeway or sympathy to any pleas for more time or complaints about not having enough resources for the task. This attitude permeated negotiations of service-level agreements between the finance business side of the house and Sally and her IT counterparts. "We-they" language was used in discussing a recent impasse and misunderstanding about due dates. In negotiations for a due date, both Finance and IT exited the meeting with different understandings. The technology side came out with the understanding that an August due date was agreed upon. However, a formal e-mail from Finance declared a due date five months earlier. The IT people believe they are not trusted by Finance. They think Finance suspects them of deliberately padding their time and human capital resource needs at worst or of being sloppy in their calculations at best. The technology managers have agreed to return to their cost, time, and labor calculations once again to more rigorously analyze these figures for use by both "sides" in this effort.

Sally believes her failure to come out of the meeting with Finance with the date she went in with damages her and all of the Technology managers' credibility, as well as the trust of their own employees. Additionally, internal to Technology, some managers are perceived as hoarding their employees and not collaboratively sharing resources with their peers when needed. One IT manager complained that this due-date disagreement represents a fundamental inequality in the business-IT relationship. He said he feels like an "order taker" and does not have the "consultative" peer relationship he expects. "We have grossly overpromised and are now poised to underdeliver."

What do the IT managers need to do to reestablish and manage a consultative-partnership relationship with their business counterparts?

Work-life balance is also very important to Sally's Malaysian employees and is part of her performance rating. But teams dedicated to this project at all levels and all over the globe work long hours to accommodate the workday in the time zones of their counterparts. Beginning the workday with a 6:00 a.m. call on one side of the world means picking up where their counterparts are finishing off a 6:00 p.m. call in another. Though Sally tells her team members to go home or stay at home if they've taken a late-night or early-morning call, she and her management counterparts agree they are sending mixed signals. Though they tell their employees to call from home or return home midday, the managers themselves often come back into the office at 8:00 p.m. for a videoconference call. Employees also believe that if they are not seen at work, they are not seen to be working. When it comes to ranking employees, someone might be at the bottom of the bunch because he or she was not seen working.

Sally knows the team leaders around the world are not of the same mind about the importance of this issue. One manager may believe this is simply part and parcel of the job people signed up for. "This kind of work takes a certain kind of person. This is a once-in-a-lifetime career opportunity. This is just the nature of global work.

Another company may decide to deliberately locate its entire management team in one portion of the globe for the duration of the project. This team may move around the globe with the project as it is deployed. This model has its own set of problems. So be it."

Another manager may disagree. She lives in a very impoverished part of the world where there are few other options for technology specialists like herself. "Do you think that if we had another option we wouldn't take it? Our employees believe we have them over a barrel and are taking advantage of them, knowing this company is the only game in town."

Sally's case illustrates tensions inherent in any business-function relationship. But these tensions are amplified due to the complexity of the matrix organization, working and negotiating across time zones, and communicating and collaborating across cultural differences. Through the advice of seasoned mentors and trusted peers, Sally has committed to learning and applying the best practices to better influence across these boundaries.

Sally's challenges require more than her personal development. Building collaboration and managing conflicts require systemic support from senior leadership.

CONFLICT MANAGEMENT
Actions, Tools, and Best Practices

The most senior executive team must model mechanisms for managing conflict. Part of the executive leadership's role is to use the following best practices:

- *Encourage people to bring conflicts to light so they can be addressed.* Publicly reward those who surface tough topics for discussion.

- *Debate alternative perspectives reasonably.* Make time for debate and the presentation of different views, appropriate evidence, and lines of argument. Communicate the value of debate by setting up a debate process, rotating debate facilitation responsibilities, and group ground rules. Use corporate training programs, newsletters, and the informal grapevine to communicate these processes and protocols throughout the organization.

- *Highlight agreements rather than disagreements.* Shift the focus from the areas conflicting parties disagree on to the areas where they do agree.

- *Assess personal collaboration and conflict management styles as a team.* Select a conflict management assessment and discuss personal and team results as a group. Begin to discuss individual and collective assumptions about the different ways of handling conflict.

One of the most rewarding aspects of working in an international organization is the opportunity to work with people from all over the world on challenging and complex tasks. As we've just seen in our four case studies, the tensions intentionally baked into the matrix structure are coupled with the pressures of doing more with less with people who have different "software of the mind." As leaders, we can model collaboration as described in this chapter, work to manage agreement and conflict as we adapt to the demands of different cultures, and develop a common language for describing what we see and experience. This business environment also requires leaders who will develop systemic organizational supporting structures that reinforce and reward collaboration and manage conflict. Using our push-pull-how interest-based business case, leading a strong organizational culture begins with the creation of a solid business case. What is the price the organization will pay in terms of time, schedule, customer service, employee satisfaction and engagement, and ultimately, organizational performance and sustainability if we fail to build a culture of collaboration? And conversely, what will the employees, customers, shareholders, and community gain when a strong culture of collaboration is achieved?

Now that we have explored influence across boundaries from the perspective of collaboration and conflict, the final resource we will discuss is the importance of your personal network of connections.

Five

Using Your Personal Network and Connections

The people on whom you depend to get your job done internationally may be hard to find on multipage organization charts. Within an international matrix organization, where resources are meant to be reallocated based on need, people are a resource redistributed frequently. International assignments change every two to three years. The scopes of people's work roles and responsibilities fluctuate with even greater regularity. You may be able to find someone on your organization's intranet equivalent to Facebook, but that person's connection with you and your initiative will not be clearly stated. Unfortunately, the important influence relationships are never clearly displayed nor are the dots connected on complex international organization charts.

With each change—or more likely, piling on—of assignment, your dependencies will fluctuate. You will always want to be asking yourself, "Who *is* the person on whom I depend today?" and "Where did the person I depended on yesterday go so I can keep in touch with him if I need him again?"

To help you with these questions, we will insert a very different picture into our image of formal relationships on an organization chart. To understand the informal relationships that defy the formal reporting boundaries of a matrix organization, step outside. Step away from your computer and go outside on the next clear, dark night. Look up. The massive display of stars is your informal relationship-oriented international organization. The connections of the various stars into constellations are your different sets of networks. The possible number of connections between networks is exponential.

Your personal network has value: social capital. This is the power of knowing the person on the other end of the line will pick up the phone when they see your caller ID. How can knowing the social network within your organization help you deliver results? Your appreciation for its power will help you understand how work actually gets done.

For information about and connections to helpful resources, you will depend on your network. Your network has nothing to do with your position or title. Initially it's not even about choosing the kinds of people you would really like to work with.

Keep in mind that strategic positioning is knowing the landscape and where you want to position your initiative, idea, or product. It is about learning which decision makers or their advisors you need to influence. Networking is the informal constellation that will help connect you to the people that the decision maker turns to for trusted and unbiased advice and subject-matter expertise. Networking helps you get exclusive information that is not readily accessible, bypass formal communication chains, take shortcuts, and save time and money by not going down culs-de-sac and taking wrong turns.

This chapter offers insight into the research and practice of identifying, developing, and maintaining relationships with others who are valuable resources for information or support. Practical tools are presented to help you optimize your professional network and make favorable connections with people from a variety of functional, regional, and business perspectives to obtain resources, information, and credibility necessary to influence others to deliver results.

Big Picture Scan

Before you read on, answer these questions:

- Do you know whom decision makers turn to for advice?

- Are you considered a trusted source of information, endorsements, or referrals?

- Does your work require unbiased analysis and interpretation of information from sources you can trust?

- Do you know people who are better positioned than you to influence people whose support you need?

- Do important decision makers, subject-matter experts, or people with resources whose cooperation you need open the e-mails or return telephone calls of people you trust and depend on?

- Do important decision makers, subject-matter experts, or people with resources you and others might need open *your* e-mails and return *your* telephone calls?

- Is your network of connections and relationships diverse?

- Do you use your network to receive and share information in a wide variety of contexts or interest groups?

- Do you have a personal code of conduct about how you use your network and the networks of others?

- Do you deliberately carve out time to make new connections on a variety of interests and nurture or reconnect with existing relationships?

Just as the matrix organization is designed to nurture the depth of expertise to be shared across the breadth of the company, so should you be nurturing the depth of your connections within functions and businesses and the breadth of your network across the organization and outside it. There are as many ways of cultivating your network as the individuals who comprise it. Your network of connections is a very personal and very valuable resource. It is your personal Wikipedia of real people who know or can find the answers to your questions.

Influence, Results, and Networks

You have a lot in common with the external entrepreneur when you are trying to deliver results in a complex organizational environment. Both of you rely on your personal network of contacts to favorably position your idea or initiative within an organization or market so that it is recognized and accepted. Entrepreneurial research calls this "gaining legitimacy." The first people you gain legitimacy with are the people you know best and who trust you.

Whether they're inside or outside an organization, those who deliver results in a complex business environment rely on their personal network of connections to reach the people who have resources and information they need to get their job done. It's all about relationships. You have people you turn to for advice and who sway your opinion. Likewise, you want to reach the trusted advisors of the people you are trying to influence. You need to understand the network of connections and relationships of the people you ultimately want to influence. Your objective is to create connections through your network to the networks of others until you reach your target.

It would be so nice if we could just walk up to members of an executive committee and ask them, "Whom do you trust and rely on for advice?" You may be surprised by their answers. You may find this trusted advisor is not someone in the organization but someone they have met socially who has subject-matter expertise. This person does not have the same biases of someone in the organization about which way a decision goes. This trusted advisor may show up in your web search as the secretary of the local society for animal welfare—a shared interest and source of the original connection.

In this way, your network is exponential—it's a constellation of your network connecting to the networks of others. You do not need to have a contact list of hundreds of connections. You do need relationships with people who have trusted relationships with others who will introduce you to or connect you with the next person in your steppingstone influence strategy. Your connections and theirs will create a bridge to the kinds of people you need to stay informed.

Remember, your message delivered by a trusted advisor or opinion leader is much more powerful than an e-mail or letter coming from you or someone the recipient doesn't know. You will want to connect with those people who are better positioned to influence the people you want to influence. Then your goal is to discuss how they might be willing to help you in your efforts. Together you may draft a message that they feel comfortable sharing with one of the people you are targeting in your influence steppingstone strategy.

Your network provides a source of information and access to people who have resources and who influence decision makers. Those with a strong network of connections say they are able to acquire access to people they would not have access to on their own, access to resources they need at a reduced price, and faster access—saving time and money—to help locate and evaluate opportunities. Through your network you will be exposed to a wide range of information about a diversity of topics—internal organizational trends or hot topics, external regional or industry trends, promising new business practices and opportunities, markets for selling your goods and services, and professional and subject-matter experts with knowledge, skills, and abilities they can offer.

There are many reasons to network. People who network report they identify 50 percent of their new ideas from their networks.[1] Your network plays a critical role in three key innovation processes: discovering opportunities, securing resources, and gaining legitimacy. Whenever you realize you have a question, an opportunity, or a problem you cannot handle on your own—whether you are an individual in a 250,000-employee international organization or an entrepreneur trying to bring a new product into a new market—you know you require the capabilities and knowledge that no one person or one source will have.

Research shows that these networking patterns are the same in all countries. The only differences are in the size of the networks and the time spent networking.[2] For example, studies of Japanese networks show that they are very small but very tight knit and are contacted very frequently.

Forming a Sustainable Network of Relationships

During times of intense organizational change, it is always good to know who the opinion leaders are so that you can learn what people are saying about change. In this case, a network of opinion leaders is used as a source of information. Alternatively, you may also use your network to send a message. The goal of your network is to connect yourself to the people you want to influence so you can present your messages of influence to them—or to the people they trust and whose advice they are likely to respect and consider and to be influenced by themselves.

A benefit of having the organizational know-how and political savvy skills we discussed in chapter 1 is that you gain insight into who the opinion leaders are, who the key decision makers are, and whom those decision makers are most likely to consult before making a decision. Connecting to these opinion leaders and trusted advisors is a networking goal.

How to Build a Network

To succeed with any initiative, seasoned business professionals know they will require different contacts and resources as their initiative evolves. Their network evolves as their initiative evolves, beginning with close, strong ties that are embedded in their social life—family, friends, and close colleagues.[3] Their network is built, sustained, and nurtured by honoring a handful of social or unspoken rules of engagement. Those rules vary from person to person. For example, one rule may be to maintain confidentiality. Another may be that when you do something for me, I'll return the favor whenever you need it.

If you already have a healthy network, then you know people build their networks from the ground up by starting with family, friends, and the people they know well. We all connect with others naturally in the course of just getting to know others. From an instrumental or opportunistic perspective, we do this with the goal of learning how to link up with someone who has a connection that is one degree closer to our target audience. This requires having a long view, sifting through many false leads, using your best listening and relationship-building skills with each new contact, and learning people's interests and needs in order to know how you might be able to help them to begin the give-and-take of reciprocal relationships.

Networking includes a balance between two forces—relationship and opportunity. The opportunity component requires a certain willingness to exert some effort in doing a bit of mutual back scratching—I'll do for you, and maybe you'll do for me. But you are more likely to form a sustainable connection with someone—one that will persist into the future with whatever minimal personal resources you are willing to exert—if you each develop a genuine liking for each other.

CASE STUDY
Jan Didot's Success through the Power of Networks

Jan Didot claims her personal network and connections are her number one resource for delivering results. "Nothing replaces the importance of delivering results. It's all about performance. My results are what drew my first manager's attention. I recognized early on that people wanted me to be successful and wanted me to help them be successful. I also knew I would have to share the credit if I wanted repeat success." This is an example of the Matthew effect discussed in chapter 1: the more credit and recognition you receive for your performance, the more credit and recognition you will receive—in the form of better assignments, more visibility, and more recognition.

"On my last assignment, I was in way over my head." Jan said. "I had no money, only the good will of a history of doing good work and helping other people out. I was in charge of a job of massive proportions and literally had one summer intern and a part-time administrative assistant as dedicated resources. But I had the responsibility to deliver a global project with high visibility that a lot of people trusted me to deliver."

According to Jan, this is where personal networks and connections came in. "It wasn't like anyone owed me any favors at this point. But I knew enough to start by calling people I knew or had heard about with reputations for delivering and told them what I was working on. I knew the excitement of working on such a breakthrough project would appeal to their sense of challenge. I also knew they knew people who could help me, so this was my influence goal. And so it went. We each made a lot of personal calls and people really pitched in. By the end of the project I was connected directly or indirectly to every region in the world and every top specialist in his or her field. It was really exhausting for all of us."

By the end of the project, Jan had to be reminded that she never had a budget. Her network was savvy enough to know that if she didn't take this opportunity to remind the senior leadership in her report of the actual FTE expended on this project, the same people would be asked to recreate similar results without budgets. She knew the favors of networks could be stretched just so far. She knew she had a lot of credit to share. So she tallied the time and effort as best she could and submitted a budget for any similar project. The sum total of FTE expended on this project in people's discretionary time was amazing. Jan closed her report by listing the names of all those who contributed in their "spare" time—and who should be formally credited with the success of this project. She asked only that the global leader send a personal letter of thanks directly to those involved. Jan did the same.

Jan Didot's is a constellation of connections. "One contact leads to another in a variety of directions," Jan said, "and before you know it, you have a personal business social network that is truly invaluable."

In a global environment, despite the matrix structure's intention of eliminating redundancies, each country or region has someone doing much the same job with some version of the same tools and some set of information he or she depends on. Those who set about deliberately creating a more global network of connections do so to deliver on the results they are accountable for. How you fit and overlap with others in your organization will depend in large part on your network and your strategic global positioning systems discussed in chapter 1. Your network is your social search engine designed to find the information and resources you need. The reward for your networking efforts is that you get what you need to do your job and meet new and interesting colleagues in the process.

Wider recognition and reward may come when you institutionalize your social connections so others don't have to reinvent your search. For example, you may invite people from within your network to convene to tackle an issue or create an opportunity together—face to face or via groupware. This takes a step toward sustainability—creating an infrastructure that can support itself and provide value to future generations. Your innovation may improve the quality of others' work life—through participation and idea generation. The savings to the organization are more than qualitative. You can quantify the time and cost savings of creating a more scalable information-sharing process and cost sharing. You will want to report the impact of these systemic improvements to your stakeholders.

PERSONAL NETWORK AND CONNECTIONS
Actions, Tools, and Best Practices

Here are some ways to build and sustain your personal network:

- *Reframe what it means to network.* Networking is not what only gregarious people, salespeople, or diplomats do. Your network is an invaluable resource businesspeople develop to achieve goals and to deliver results. These relationships may begin superficially or with an intense interaction within a tight deadline. They may begin with a desire to explore an opportunity or to complete a transaction. However they begin, the best networks are deliberately nurtured to evolve into relationships with interesting people you infrequently see but respect and enjoy keeping in touch with. One of the most successful international managers I know who has an incredible network of connections says she doesn't work to maintain her connections at all. "They just start with people I get to know well and really like and who really like me," she told me. "I can call people I haven't talked to in years when I need to talk to them about something. I don't keep files on them or anything—just their phone numbers—and we pick up where we left off three years ago. None of them are very needy and they don't want to be stroked or contacted unless it's important. They haven't forgotten who I am."

- *Assess your current network.* Check whether you have connections both inside and outside your organization. As much as Jan depends on her network, she admits that with each new job, she expands her network in new directions. When we mapped her network (or sociogram), she discovered she reached the key decision makers or their trusted advisors and at least one subject-matter expert in every region, line of business, and functional specialty in her international organization. But now she had P&L responsibility for a product line in an entire region. She realized her network outside her organization was very limited. She decided to start that network from scratch and began by contacting her friends and family in other companies in her region within and outside her industry. Jan believed failure to have her finger on the pulse of local external trends, alternative perspectives, and business practices would severely limit her ability to drive results in this new arena.

- *Identify influential networks and mentors.* These are people who can offer opportunities to let others know about your contributions and your initiatives and who can help connect you to the decision maker's trusted advisors.

- *Diversify and broaden your current network of connections.* Take an honest look at the kinds of people you find yourself working and socializing with. If you find they are all people from your business function or product line, subject-matter experts from your industry, people from your native culture, or those who share your same interests and world-view, consider joining other conversations, applying for projects that concern a cross section of your business or community. Create the goal of forming and following up on new relationships.

- *Attend professional associations or interest group gatherings.* Select two associations and find out if your organization will pay the annual dues of either one as part of its professional development budget. Do not allow yourself any "perfectly logical excuses" not to attend meetings. If a list of attendees is available before a meeting, select a handful of individuals you might want to meet for business reasons or because of common interests. Do an Internet search to learn something about them that you are genuinely interested in—their organizations, their competition, trends in their industries. This will arm you with a sense of purpose and the prospect of satisfying a genuine curiosity. One of the best benefits of these meetings is the chance to meet people out of your natural circle and to learn something new. Take your business cards, and once at the gathering, deliberately go up to people and introduce yourself. Be prepared with a short and concise message of what it is that you do. But transition swiftly to listening. When you remember this is about building connections, not selling your product, initiative, or service, you will feel a sense of relief.

- *Follow up.* Make promises to send new contacts information or a link or an e-mail introduction to someone they may value knowing. Write your promises on the back of their business cards and quickly fulfill your promises. Send an e-mail thank-you note or a "nice to meet you" message.

- *Create a memory aid to remember and acknowledge personal details about your contacts if something really stood out for you in your conversations with this person.* Jan's early work exposure to a few executives who called her by name made a big impression on her, so she made a career out of addressing people personally and by name. Jan naturally refers to family, children, and anything else to show appreciation for the people she knows and depends on. When people ask Jan for career advice, she buys them a cup of coffee, asks them to tell her about themselves, and listens. Jan calls her networking style a "roots up" approach. "In my call center days I would position myself by the front door and say hello to the incoming people and good-bye to the outgoing shifts to be visible."

If you think it will be useful, add minimal information about the people you meet and talk with alongside their contact information in your computer contact list. Write any pertinent details—for example, the place you met, what they were working on at the time, what they did for you, their personal interests, the ages of their children or the colleges they are attending, and what their family situation is.

- *Enhance the depth of your network.* Specialize your connections to increase the depth of your understanding of, expertise in, or efficiency of delivering products and services. Attend ongoing knowledge-sharing forums or communities of practice with colleagues from the specialized professional interest within or outside your organization.

- *Enhance the breadth of your network.* Develop a broader perspective and build business awareness through short-term or long-term organization-wide improvement projects with colleagues from across the organization. Volunteer to attend discussions and organizational activities that will put you in contact with colleagues in different businesses who have different business experiences or different regional experiences.

- *Convert your existing contacts into potential sources of information and resources.* Reconnect with people you already know to update them on what you are working on. Let them know what some of your challenges are or that you are in search of information about best practices, research, or experts on a subject. Inquire what they are working on and offer to help them whenever you are able.

■ *Use your network to create a personal board of directors.* Identify a variety of experienced individuals, mentors, advocates, and sponsors to help promote your ideas or initiatives to broaden your reach, your perspective, and your career.

■ *Connect when you are asked to connect.* When someone in your network asks you to meet someone, make every effort to do so, at least by phone, out of respect and your belief in the idea of networking. Chances are, the connection will benefit you as well as the person making the connection. You might begin by checking the person's profile on your organizational intranet. What begins with a casual talk about mutual business responsibilities will lead to the common ground your connector had in mind. You will find you can share the person's research, learn his or her approach to a problem, or even share a resource.

■ *Connect when you land in the country of your contacts.* When you are traveling on business into the offices where one of your connections works, give that person a call. Make it one of your rules, as a way of thanking and showing appreciation for your relationship, to connect when you're traveling, no matter how tired or busy you are.

■ *Be the connector: don't wait for the organization to connect you.* Remember, people throughout the global organization are doing what you are doing in some form. People who have their heads down doing the work do not always know others are working to solve the same dilemma or deliver the same results. They need someone to pull them together, save each other time and money, and provide relationships in the process. Don't wait for the organization to do this for you. Make it happen. The more people you tell what you are doing, the more individuals in the organization will be aware and the greater the chances someone will make a connection.

■ *Remind yourself that your network opens doors for you with access to information you need through the connections of others, knowledge of opportunities, people who can help you, and ways to acquire prod-ucts and services at a reduced cost.* Networking helps break the isolation by creating paths to others. A social network of people who know what you do or who have tried and succeeded—or failed—at doing what you are doing can help validate your cur-rent reality (i.e., "I'm not the only one"). Your network of peers will help you solve problems and avoid reinventing the wheel. In short, a solid professional network can help you feel con-nected in the wide world of a large organization and manage stress while being more effective in your job.

What Can Top Management Do?

Top management can eliminate systemic barriers to networking and create formal practices that support networking.

- *Connect male managers as mentors with female managers.* According to one study, "When a well-placed individual who possesses greater legitimacy (often a male) takes an interest in a woman's career, her efforts to build social capital can proceed more effi-ciently."[4] Research shows women are much less networked than men. According to a study of management behavior, women are far more likely to be task oriented beyond the normal busi-ness hours. Men, on the other hand, are more likely to spend their extra hours networking with other men.[5] Research shows women are less networked because they do not make network-ing a priority. They make home life their priority. This is why some organizations still promote women's networking fo-rums—and not men's networking forums. Organizations can help women appreciate why networking and building social capital deserves more attention.

- *Ensure that employees on international teams are encouraged to net-work—and have time to devote to the development of their profes-sional networks.* A reality of international work crossing global time zones means everyone makes calls that do not fit within a ten-hour block of time dedicated to work. Early-morning and late-night calls are the norm. However, many managers who are on these late-night and early-morning calls report they still believe their performance is being measured on "face time" in the office rather than on their performance. In organizations with a highly competitive forced-ranking performance rating system, managers and individual team members alike fear that not being seen in the office will negatively impact their ranking.[6]

- *Uncover mixed signals within middle management that work against work-life balance and networking.* In a recent leadership conference, the manager who won the Manager of the Year award was praised for her selfless and tireless work ethic. In a later large-group discussion, another manager praised the award recipient for her performance but rejected the emphasis on her working until 2:00 a.m. many days. A debate ensued that was resolved in favor of round-the-clock availability. Top managers who value networks as a core component to delivering results can do their part in making introductions, referring connections, and expressing their feelings regarding its importance.

- *Promote the idea of ad hoc forums for generating ideas.* Establish yearly cross-region peer collaboration forums or communities of practice forums for more than just the most senior leadership. Dedicate one week a year as a peer innovation forum for which employees submit a 250-word proposal for a five-minute presentation and five-minute question-and-answer session for cross-fertilization of ideas, name recognition, and follow-up collaboration. All this can be done remotely via videoconferencing and using groupware, but the face-to-face connection is invaluable.

- *Hold yourself to having one "public relations" day every week and get out and walk around the building you work in so people have exposure and informal connections with you.* Have coffee at the coffee bar in your building or in a busy hall. Once a week, do not have coffee or lunch brought into a private meeting. Have the meeting in the company cafeteria. Make a point of listening to one employee and suggest one person that employee should connect with.

Your personal network of connections will provide you with the fastest link to up-to-date information, an introduction to a subject-matter expert you need to talk to, and access to resources your current budget cannot afford. No other communication vehicle in your international business can connect you more quickly to the people on your steppingstone strategy to take you one step closer to meeting your influence goals. Because of their relationship with you, people in your network will give you their resources, their free time to talk about an issue of importance to you, alternative perspectives, and advice about best practices you were unaware of. Your network is one of your most valuable and critical resources for influencing across international boundaries to deliver your promises for results.

Pulling It All Together

Since the beginning of this book, five key resources for succeeding in a global business environment have been described and illustrated as discrete resources—individual parts removed from the whole for close examination and understanding. Each resource offered actions, tools, and best practices to apply to better deliver the results for which you are responsible. You also have insights into the unique challenges and predictable dilemmas of doing business within an international matrix organization.

The following case illustrates the power of integrating the resources required to influence across boundaries. In this story you will trace how Dee Shekhar's use of strategic positioning (organizational know-how, political savvy, stakeholder communication, and the ability to sustain change), cross-cultural know-how, personal influence and persuasion, collaboration and conflict management, and networking led to her ability to achieve dramatic results in a challenging and complex international environment.

So that you recognize and may borrow Dee's best practices, throughout this case, we'll refer to the resource Dee employs in parentheses at the end of a paragraph.

CASE STUDY
Dee Shekhar and the Ability to Influence Across Boundaries

Dee Shekhar knew that private individuals were beginning to set up their own private schools as alternatives to public schools in sub-Saharan countries. From experience, she knew private and public schools in developing countries are not like what one expects in developed countries. The public schools in a sub-Saharan country, for example, may be funded out of the local municipal or ministerial budget but may receive no funds at all for facilities or even for basic supplies. Often some level of corruption and very little accountability exist. The public schools are run by civil servants and have no sanctions for teachers failing to show up for a day's work. They may have no money to replace light bulbs or provide textbooks. (Strategic positioning, influence and persuasion: preparatory evidence for the push strategy)

The quality of education may be so poor that a parent or concerned member of the community—usually a woman—with immense passion for children and a strong belief in the opportunity created by education would decide to set up a private school on her own. This behavior was consistent with Dee's knowledge of this region's culture—the common history throughout sub-Saharan Africa of both colonization and slavery. The region is characterized by cultural norms of collectivism, interdependence, and suppression of self-interests; reciprocity—the exchange of favors; a close association with the earth; and the belief in symbiotic, mutually beneficial relationships.[1] (Cross-cultural know-how: dimensions of culture)

The private schools Dee visited were set up in a garage or in a makeshift collection of unsafe structures made of remnants of materials collected over time. They were clearly not built to any building codes or safety standards. Construction was never-ending, so children came to school and played on an open construction site with dangerous building debris around them.

Private schools had more in common than their meager setup. Their instruction was precarious because of unstable income. Children may be unable to have any practical science labs because the school had run out of money to finish construction of the science laboratory. These little private schools had no accreditation, no quality controls, and no ability to have more systematic and orderly capital growth. The teacher-owners were funded in dribs and drabs.

Dee knew that what she witnessed in this one city in one country was replicated throughout a number of developing countries, not just in the sub-Saharan region. She believed she had a solution with tremendous benefit to children and to the educational and banking systems on a local and sustainable basis. If these small private schools had access to affordable financing, they could better plan their construction projects and focus on delivering consistent instruction to the children. She knew that if she could make her idea work in this one city, it could be replicated throughout sub-Saharan Africa. (Strategic positioning: the ability to sustain change)

Dee Shekhar operated within an international organization of internal complexity, bureaucracy, intentional overlap, and stakeholder communication requirements. With this came external interdependencies, interest groups, regulatory oversight of high visibility, rigorous compliance standards, and stringent written reporting requirements. Dee believed that even within a highly bureaucratic organization such as this, there was actually an awful lot of room for independence to get a lot done by flying under the radar. "I knew a lot about the existing systems, policies, and support structures. I knew that nothing I was doing was brand new. It was more a synthesis—creating new things out of old parts. I knew I just had to know where to look." Dee knew this project fit into her organization's overall mission of building social infrastructure and targeting the poorest of the poor countries. Africa was a huge focus. And everyone who learned of this project immediately recognized it would not be a one-off project and knew it could be replicated in many developing countries in Africa. (Strategic positioning: organizational know-how, political savvy)

Dee started by determining whose cooperation she would need: a local bank, a few private school leaders, local educational ministries or associations, and technical assistance facilities that she knew existed in this country. As for costs, she assumed she would be allocated no budget for this project. She would use her free time and imagination to work the potential of this project at a very micro level. Anyone she recruited would have to work on this during his or her own time. Her trips to Africa would have to come out of her manager's budget—which could easily afford two trips at the very least. (Strategic positioning: steppingstone strategy; collaboration and conflict management; networking know-how)

"When I proposed this project to my director," Dee said, "he was skeptical of my chances. He was supportive, however, and granted my time as well as a lot of leeway throughout the project." In Dee's experience in leading innovation, this kind of benign neglect on the part of her managers was a recurring theme, and their trust and noninterference was just the kind of support she needed. (Strategic positioning: organizational know-how and political savvy)

Fundamentally, Dee's vision for the project was predicated on the belief that private schools needed help with financing capital improvements. If they could have an assured source of funds to cover their building projects, construction would be orderly, and costs would be contained because construction teams and equipment would not need to be mobilized and demobilized. Dee's work was to find someone to lend them that cash. These loans, if sized right, could help ease some of the cash-flow problems that the schools faced. More importantly, they could free up the owners' attention to focus on teaching and not on where the next payment installment to the contractor would come from. Providing such small loans directly would be terribly expensive—the transaction costs of structuring and delivering individual loans of $100,000 or even less would be prohibitive for Dee's organization. So a local bank needed to be induced to provide such loans—and the incentive would be a guarantee from Dee's organization for such loans. (Strategic positioning: stakeholder communication; influence and persuasion: peripheral influence strategy)

"I had to assemble a team but had no budget to pay anyone," Dee said. "Once I got my director's agreement, I talked about this incessantly. I was so passionate about the immediate needs of these schools and the education of these children. The purpose touched so many people on so many levels. From a pragmatic, sustainable, and mission-based perspective, the payoffs and leveragability of this very simple process were obvious to everyone." (Strategic positioning: sustainable change; influence and persuasion: peripheral influence—vision and higher purpose; collaboration: focus on collective results; networking)

Dee knew she would be recruiting from within an international organization full of the brightest and the best who were very values driven. Many of them came from developing countries around the world and had extensive exposure to the conditions within developing countries. "I knew I would need an investment officer," Dee said. "One of the investment officers in the regional office saw the staggering need and potential replication of this effort and agreed to help me with the follow-up, report writing, and appraisal. Yori introduced me to Catrin, whose local presence and personal network of connections were a great boon to selling the project in country, and she was instrumental in getting the needed technical assistance out to the schools." (Networking)

The manager of the regional office was personally delighted to be credited with this innovative and interesting project, and he offered both Yori and Catrin to work on the project. Dee also reached out to Amelia, who was a key contributor to a South American project they had worked on together and was a seasoned, adaptable, and sharp professional. Another friend who was a lawyer agreed to write the final loan agreement. He too saw the replication potential and knew that he was making an investment in time that would pay off in the future. According to Dee, "This project somehow captured the imagination of everyone who worked on it and everyone became very personally motivated to see it happen. Another attractive feature—the team was truly an integrated headquarter/regional one which was in keeping with our global-local mind-set." (Strategic positioning:

193

organizational know-how, political savvy, and the ability to sustaining change; influence and persuasion: peripheral influence—vision and higher purpose)

Dee set about anticipating and overcoming the objections of the local bank by describing what a private school is from a practical and logical perspective. Most parents do not move their child on a whim, so these schools would not be opening and closing haphazardly. Once a child was admitted, chances were very high that he or she would stay for the duration. Also, parents make regular monthly payments to the school—a steady and predictable cash flow to pay teachers, buy school supplies, and service any debt. (Influence and persuasion: central influence)

Dee knew that if the local bank would work with the small private schools, it could also handle tuition receivables—parents could be required to deposit their monthly fees directly. Having the parents coming into the bank to make their monthly payments would create monthly foot traffic of potential new clients. The bank could also offer other services to the school, like handling teacher payroll. From a community development and sustainability perspective, this additional activity at the bank level would help develop the banking sector in the region as well and bring more people into the formal economy. Also, with a loan guaranteed by Dee's company's AAA-rated balance sheet and the possibility of technical assistance to create bankable business plans, the local bank could create a whole new line of business, enhance its reputation in the local market, and possibly enjoy better credit ratings on its future ventures. (Influence and persuasion: central influence—the how influence strategy; collaboration)

Dee also knew that sustainable change requires technical assistance. The private schools needed more than just money. For this initiative to be sustainable beyond the first infusion of cash, the private schools' leaders would need to learn how to be business owners and would need technical assistance in the form of training and development in business planning, enrollment planning, bookkeeping, and cash-flow management. The teachers would need sufficient material and pedagogical support to provide quality teaching. The schools would benefit from external accreditation to demonstrate that they meet certain standards to increase their value proposition. (Strategic positioning: the ability to sustain change)

Sustainability also requires external recognition and support. These private schools would require accreditation to be recognized within and outside their community. To that end, Dee's project included technical assistance to the Independent Schools Association to help set standards for the private schools. The Independent Schools Association standards could be a recognized "stamp of approval" the private schools would seek to attain. The association was required to focus equally on the smallest schools—not only the largest. (Strategic positioning: political savvy and the ability to sustain change)

Because of her thorough knowledge of her organization, Dee knew special donor funds existed just for these kinds of small programs in less-developed regions of the world, including sub-Saharan Africa. Many of these programs focused on helping small and medium enterprises (SMEs)—very often the backbone of the private sector in these countries—develop business plans, seek financing, and professionalize their operations. Dee's big insight was that a small private school was no different from any other small and medium enterprises—and so tools and support available for other SMEs could just as readily be channeled to private schools. Bringing private schools into the recognized formal language and structures of the organization was a small but critical element to win and stabilize this initiative. (Strategic positioning: organizational know-how)

When the project was delivered, it was a resounding success.

Dee's organization approved giving the local bank a risk-sharing facility that would share in losses on the school loan portfolio should a private school fail to repay. The investment officer who inherited this project from Dee reported that the project did well. The bank started a second one in that country and one in another African country and is considering others. A technical assistance specialist from Dee's group later joined the team to further develop and flesh out the technical assistance requirements, and this program was successfully presented to aid agencies for financing.

One of the first staunch skeptics to oppose this project quickly changed his tune when Dee and her team achieved success. He talked up the project, promoted it, presented it, and became the public face of the project. Dee ceded formal organizational recognition to him but won the appreciation of the people who actually worked alongside her. Dee believes that a lot of underground currency exists in the absence of formal recognition by the organization. She chose to focus on her broad base of support from an execution perspective. (Strategic positioning: political savvy—sharing credit—and stakeholder communication)

Dee said, "Once at a work celebration I did casually and with humor remind the skeptic of his original resistance to this project he now lauded. He acknowledged me by saying, 'Everybody knows your reputation, and you are held in very high regard.'"

Dee's story illustrates how she was able to deliver results using the five influence resources of strategic positioning, cross-cultural know-how, influence and persuasion, collaboration and conflict management, and networking. She influenced change across the complexities of international boundaries—within her own organization's global-local structure; between and among nongovernment organizations, private small businesses, public agencies, and private banks; and with stakeholders with diverse interests and dimensions of culture.

Dee considers herself adept in innovating on the sidelines but less effective inside a highly political bureaucracy. She is passionately curious and loves the challenge of solving international business challenges but recognizes when she neglects any one of this handful of resources. She considers herself an apt and eager student, and her use of and strength in any one resource depends on the challenges of each unique situation.

This is a recurring theme among international leaders who influence across boundaries. As in Dee's case, the experiences of many successful international leaders validate this handful of resources—and these leaders admit that the particular resource emphasized varies from assignment to assignment. For example, Jan felt her network of connections pulled her through on her first major international assignment without dedicated budget or resources, but her ability to collaborate and manage conflict in her current assignment is now being tested. Another international manager felt his cross-cultural know-how benefited him greatly in building relationships and commitment in his Southeast Asia assignment, but his current challenge is to strategically position his initiative and his team in Vancouver. Another manager's relationship-centered influence skills were at first of little use to him while he dealt with the culture shock of doing business for the first time in a matrix organization. The reality of having regional, functional, and global project managers to report to, a team scattered around the world, and stakeholders with competing interests overwhelmed his e-mail in-box. He literally forgot to pick up the phone.

DEVELOPING YOUR ABILITY TO INFLUENCE ACROSS BOUNDARIES
Setting Goals and Planning Actions

Each new global assignment will require a creative synthesis of these resources—a recombination of ingredients to suit the tastes and requirements of each new cultural business setting. As you hone your strengths and record high performance using these resources, your choices will expand and become clearer.

Your continued success requires continued learning and self-development. This demands the engagement of your mind, body, and spirit:

- Your ability to think rationally and relationally; your cross-cultural intelligence to effectively collaborate with others; and your business, organizational, and political savvy to effectively maneuver, strategize, and deliver results within a networked international business community you must create for yourself

- Your physical ability to adjust what you look like, sound like, and say as you encounter others with different dimensions of culture; convey a personal presence of authority, authenticity, and approachability; and build the physical stamina of working harder and longer across time zones

- Your spirit, self-confidence, and motivation to persevere in the face of multiple and often competing directives and projects and to appreciate your resilience and courage to redouble your efforts with each wrong turn, failure, and cultural gaffe

The challenges and rewards of being successful in your international work count on your personal interest in and motivation to be challenged by an ever-changing environment, clarity of personal values and goals, and a strong sense of self—knowing who you are even as you adjust to meet the needs of different cultures and shifting work demands.

Belief in Self and Goal Setting

The challenge for all of us who want to succeed in the global business environment is to integrate these five resources into actions appropriate to the demands of each assignment. Armed with these resources and insights, you are better equipped to identify and choose which situations you are most likely to be successful in—and to set as goals those assignments for which you are not best suited while you develop and prepare. You may decide you are not ready to take that four-foot water jump with your dream horse yet, but you may decide to build up to this goal through training and a series of tests as a novice rider over creek beds with a well-trained schooling horse. It is important to set goals at an appropriately challenging "stretch" level and to implement suitable actions, tools, and best practices to achieve those goals.

Self-efficacy is the belief you have in yourself to accomplish a goal. This belief in self is itself motivating and will affect the kinds of goals and the level of goals you set for yourself. You anticipate success—and even as you anticipate the false starts and failures you may encounter, you remember the times when you brushed yourself off and returned to the game and succeeded. Goal setting and self-efficacy go together.

The goal in the case of this book is to sharpen your resources to deliver initiatives of strategic importance within a complex matrix organization in a global business environment. Now that you know what that means, you know this is a really high goal that not everyone or every team is cut out for.

This book makes the case that in order to attain this goal, you need to master strategic positioning, cross-cultural know-how, influence and persuasion, collaboration and conflict management, and networking. This is a very tall order. The higher the goal, the harder and smarter you and your team will have to work to achieve it.

Begin by assessing which of the five resources your current and future "dream" position or success requires and where you can place yourself to make a greater contribution. This book has focused on interdependence and collaboration, which means working with others to achieve goals. Which resources are most critical and most likely to be challenged in fulfilling this mission in the short, medium, and long terms?

As you read this book, some of the resources resonated more than others: "That's what I've been missing" or "That's why that worked so well" or "I haven't been making such a mess of things after all." Review the "Big Picture Scan" at the beginning of each resource chapter and select the resources you most want to develop. Check your personal level of confidence in your ability to develop each of the five resource areas. What personal strengths, changes, and adjustments will the mastery of each of the five resources require of you and of those on whom you depend?

This scan will lead you to develop realistic yet challenging goals. Knowing that personal growth is in order, select the actions, tools, and best practices offered in each chapter.

Having worked with hundreds of international business leaders at all levels, I have come to appreciate the importance of high self-efficacy. It is due to high self-confidence that leaders are willing to take the risks challenging tasks often entail. You see this personally in areas where you believe in yourself—the greater your belief in yourself, the greater your commitment to a goal, the better you will work, and the longer you will persist and persevere. You've seen this same principle at work on a team level as well. A multinational team will commit, work harder, and persist when its members have a clear sense of identity and efficacy as a group. This team identity and sense of direction due to high-reaching goals will serve it well in an uncertain global business environment that requires adaptability and flexibility.

The purpose of this book is to provide you with new insights, a practical understanding of the global organization in which you work, and tools you can use immediately to be successful. Within the matrix organization you will share your formal management privileges with many others. The collective mind-set of the matrix is an advantage for those who are determined to work well with others. The opportunity to meet and collaborate with people from around the world to achieve a goal is the best kind of world travel. When you open your head, heart, and mind to the rich experience of participating in the activities of daily living with people of cultures from around the globe, you get to see the world through another's eyes.

You have had the chance to read the stories of people like you who deliver results across geographic, cultural, and international business boundaries and who must influence a high degree of cooperation to deliver results without direct control, formal authority, or position power. I hope you have found in their stories ways to develop your own personal network and strategy to effectively influence, communicate with, and align diverse business partners. Though the five resources of international influence have been discussed individually, in application, you will combine these resources to complement and overlap each other.

I learned that designing the right organizational structure on paper or the best architecture and operating model with the counsel of the best information-systems research scientists is one thing. But delivering results within successive waves of organizational transformation globally is quite another. I hope that each time you will find the right action, tool, or best practice you need right now to influence across boundaries and build lasting connections.

 **Appendix A**

Scanning the Big Picture

Success in a complex international organization begins with a thorough understanding of the terrain or landscape or setting in which you will be working. Before you set out on your journey of delivering results, you will want to get the lay of the land and anticipate any boundaries you will need to cross.

When considering the future direction of their organizations, leadership teams spend considerable time understanding the setting or terrain—whether by region or globally—in which a particular product or line of business will compete. Depending on the thoroughness of last year's scan, this year's analysis of the environment may be checking to see what changes took place since the previous year. Creating the most accurate and up-to-date assessment of the "outside" encourages leaders to retest the feasibility and goodness of their "inside" vision, strategy, and structure.

What is a "scan"? A scan is a thorough examination. We're all familiar with body scans at airports or CAT scans at a hospital. A scan can also be a quick glance. A great way to think of a scan is as both the image of an initial thorough examination or inspection and a repeated cursory glance to confirm earlier findings.

As part of a strategic thinking and planning process, four scans are conducted. Leadership teams begin with a scan of the external environment or the context in which the business will compete to anticipate threats and opportunities. A scan of the company's internal environment is conducted to analyze the company's capacity to compete. These two environmental scans provide a shared set of planning assumptions.

One element of the internal organizational scan is an evaluation of the leaders who are currently in place. Do they have the ability to lead in the international marketplace within a complex organization? What are the strengths and depth of the current leadership who must influence, direct, align, and motivate others to execute the strategy and achieve goals?

The third scan is a personal scan. What is your *personal* ability to influence across boundaries—your strengths and weaknesses in the resources you will need?

A critically important fourth scan is your scan of the individuals and collective audiences you will seek to influence. Elements of this fourth scan and ways to influence diverse audiences have been discussed in depth throughout this book and are summarized in appendix D because this scan is the cornerstone of influence.

Why scan? Think of team sports. Obviously, any competitive sports team will want to know as much as possible about the team they are playing against. But they will also want to know what the playing field looks like, what kind of weather is forecasted, and any other conditions that favor their strengths or pose threats to their weak spots. They'll want to know who will be enforcing certain rules off the field, who paid for tickets (and what they expect in order to feel they got their money's worth), and who's sponsoring the team with investment for uniforms, practice equipment, and capital improvements to their home field.

The greater the uncertainty about the quality of the information about their competitor, the weather, field conditions, and fan enthusiasm, the more unpredictable the team's outcome. The team will need to develop multiple strategies or game plans and different lineups or structures designed and tested for effectiveness.

Successful corporate leaders regularly examine the current and anticipated future trends inside and outside their organizations to ensure reality jibes with their most ideal scenario of consecutive winning seasons.

Performing external, internal, and leadership scans or examinations results in a shared sense of the context in which a leader or leaders will compete and deliver results. A shared understanding of the external environment and its implications for an organization creates a shared set of assumptions that guide decisions about the strategy and structure that will do the best in that environment.

The external scan helps answer why the competitive business environment is moving in one direction rather than another. This scan will help you more thoroughly understand why your industry is changing—or should change—and what is occurring within the target market or markets of your business.

Doing these scans with your team will create a shared understanding of the specific elements in the external environment that have a direct impact on your organization and, by direct extension, on your team. This kind of collective activity will engage your entire team in broadening and lengthening their perspective—a critical thinking skill essential to strategic and cultural intelligence.

SCANNING TOOLS
Select Your Instruments before Proceeding

A shift in perspective is critical thinking, a process of disciplined reflection, and requires some preparation. A useful analogy to set the stage for a scan is to first acknowledge that different kinds of scans require different kinds of lenses and optical tools. In order to be prepared for a particular scanning operation, the proper instruments must be at hand. For example, a scan of the global economy would require a satellite in order to take in the entire global context. If you want to look at trends in a specific industry that might occur over the next fifteen to twenty years, a telescope provides a focused but faraway perspective. Binoculars would be more appropriate if your planning horizon is in the nearer term, say, only twelve to eighteen months ahead. If your initiative is dependent upon the results of many other initiatives and decisions outside your control, a wide-angle lens takes in a broader view. A magnifying glass is designed to examine one item carefully and is best suited for the team's analysis of a single customer group, competitor, stakeholder, or incentive policy. When a particular balance sheet item, personnel issue, or customer behavior is of interest, a microscope examines the minute detail and might prove most useful.

As you shift perspective or need your team to shift perspective from broad, strategic, long-term thinking to more tactical, immediate thinking, let your team know which lens you are using. This will promote the use of a common language and demonstrate the importance of moving in and out of a strategic or tactical perspective.

You will want to get two other items in order before beginning your first scan: trend and horizon. If you are looking at trends in the external and internal environments, for example, everyone should have a shared understanding of what constitutes a trend. Simply speaking, a trend is something that is occurring now that you believe will continue to occur into the future. Little will be gained by a more expert or analytical definition. To jump-start thinking about trends, you may want to ask those who are participating in these scans to bring "artifacts" that provide clues or evidence that a trend is building. Consider yourself an archeologist digging up clues about an ancient culture. In the archeology of today's business environment, clues or evidence might take the form of copies of recent policies or regulations, news clippings, e-mails, memos, reports, photographs, or headlines from relevant publications. When the scan is scheduled, include the request for tangible and everyday evidence of external and internal trends.

Another useful starting agreement is the planning horizon. Before you begin the scan, imagine a journey where you see the curve of the horizon, the point that separates the visible earth from the sky. From this day, this point of departure, the horizon represents the journey's end point or point of arrival. How far into the future will we be looking? Twenty years? Five years? Three years? Twelve months? One CEO of an international organization said he believed the horizon was determined by how long it would take to produce a new product or service or to turn the organization in a new direction. His planning horizon was eighteen months, though he thought in terms of quarterly earnings.

The volatility or uncertainty of the environment in which an organization operates may shorten planning to the extent that a year feels distant and far away. In one international development organization, the planning horizon was much longer. Development experts considered how long it would take to build a self-sustaining system—its self-funding, infrastructure, training to change mind-sets, and an educational foundation. An international shipbuilder looked fifteen to twenty years out because its leaders' experience told them it would take that long to turn around to design, build, and outfit a new ship. In the business world, three to five years is a very common planning horizon.

A common understanding of the tools to be used in the scan, what constitutes a trend, and the agreed-upon planning horizon are about all you need to start a scan.

SCAN ONE
The Big Picture

The first scan looks at the business environment from an external perspective. An accurate environmental scan not only informs the leaders' vision for their company's successful future but helps them create realistic strategies; design the business structure and operating model; develop adequate support mechanisms to sustain change; and select, develop, and retain the top talent for winning. A first scan might examine trends like these that have an effect on people and businesses around the world:

- The global economic upheaval of recession, market turbulence, diminished spending capacity, tight belts, low investor confidence, wait-and-see, and high uncertainty. High unemployment, increased demand for social services, and diminished public funding for those social services. The resulting pervasive global social fear and anxiety, frustration, and mistrust of and anger at banks and investment and financial institutions of any sort. A hunkering-down attitude of saving over spending that reaches around the world.

- More knowledgeable, outspoken, and sophisticated consumers and active shareholders and nations legislating increased regional oversight, resulting in powerful and stringent regulatory and compliance functions. Terrorism, warfare, civil unrest, gangsterism, and fraud, which heighten concerns for personal, property, and identity and institutional security and promote the emergence of an industry geared to ensuring personal, property, and identity security.

- Universal expectations for instantaneous connection and online information, which have pushed technology as the premier solution for business transactions and social interaction. The demand for greener business, home, and personal consumption.

After a look at global trends, the next step is to delve into the trends in your unique regional or global business environment. For example, Michael George, president and CEO of QVC, recently stated that China's stringent regulations of the use of China's airwaves will put on hold QVC's hopes of penetrating the world's largest market.[1] A financial services company may look to the social climate of distrust and decide to exit the mortgage business altogether for fear of jeopardizing or risking its customers' loyalty to its brand. The demographic trending of an aging population may signal a shift in product and service mixes. The viewing habits within market segments as compared to other viewing options—personal computers or hand-held digital devices, for example—will help television broadcasters determine if their industry is on an incline or decline.

To generate the greatest participation and freedom of expression, start a scan without any preset categories of trends. Ask open-ended questions such as, "What are the external trends that directly or indirectly impact our organization and that our organization must take into account when looking forward to and planning its future?" Once the ideas have been shared, the group can cluster similar items into categories.

One outcome of this scanning process is a greater understanding of the degree to which dynamics in the outside world directly or indirectly drive the decisions of your organization's leaders—which in turn directly or indirectly impact your team's ability to deliver results. This exercise promotes a more holistic or systemic frame of mind that will be essential to influencing others: "That's why we're moving in this direction" or "There's no way we can make headway with these kinds of restrictions." Rather than one individual making these connections about these realities of the external world, the collective group or team makes the connections.

Organizations often pay external business or market analysts to conduct an expert scan of the current and anticipated future trends that will impact their competitive edge. Or the marketing group may have conducted such analyses. However, the results of these studies are no substitute for a collective practice. A shared understanding and perspective is fundamental to influence.

To create a shared frame of mind, language, understanding, and perspective, you will want to plan to deliberately bring your audience, your team, your group along on the critical thinking path. This mental journey from information to understanding to action—as a group—happens when you are leading as a teacher. The group comes to understandings and realizations on their own with the leader's skilled guidance as a facilitator—no authority, no lectures, and no tests.

Following a brief discussion of the trends, ask the group to identify which trends might pose threats to your organization and which might offer opportunities. Wait until you have scanned the internal environment to weigh and prioritize these threats and opportunities.

The next link in your mental journey to a shared and strategic big-picture perspective is to examine the realities of your organization's internal environment as it is today.

SCAN TWO
Your Internal Organization

What are the internal trends that directly impact your organization's success and that must be taken into account when planning its future? The answers may include both the tangible and intangible. Whatever an individual believes will impact the future of the organization is described as it is today. The scan of the internal organization may be seen from a variety of perspectives. As in the scan of the external environment, the question of internal trends is open ended and without constraint of suggested category or variable. Leadership and management, vision and strategy, organizational structure, systems and processes, control and incentive, coaching reinforcement, emotional climate, image and reputation, culture, tools and technologies, operational support, human and capital resources—all will offer descriptions of your organization from the inside.

Envisioning the Desired Future of the Organization

Your team's scan began with an agreement of the planning time horizon (e.g., five years out, three years out, eighteen months out) and the scope of what might be included—all the regions in which your organization does business, the entire globe, or just the regions in which you and your team must deliver results. By looking at the future trends outside and inside your organization, you created a shared set of assumptions regarding what you must take into consideration when planning for your future.

Before you begin to weigh and prioritize the negative and positive impacts the different variables of the internal and external environments may have on your organization, you need a point of reference on which to base this assessment. It is easier to examine the internal and external environments more closely when you compare them with the mission or purpose of the organization and its vision of where it wants to be in the future.

Remind yourself and your team of your organization's mission or purpose, its reason for being. Next, remind yourselves of your organization's future vision. This is not its strategy or how it will achieve that vision. It is the organization's core values or principles and beliefs. It's what your organization aspires to be in the future. When a rough description of the mission or purpose of the organization and its desired future state has been discussed, the team can return to look at its scans of the external environment and its internal environment.

Focusing on the External Drivers

Given the mission and desired future state of the organization, the group now engages in a discussion of the relative impact of the external drivers on the organization. External trends are examined more closely from the perspectives of opportunity and threat. This practice of examining trends from both sides engrains the relevance of each trend in the group's mind-set.

First reexamine each influence in the external environment from a defensive position of danger, risk, and threat. Begin by asking which trends are most likely to pose a risk. Drive further into this scan by asking, "What is the single greatest threat the external environment poses to the organization?" There is no single right answer to this question. However, a very short list of the greatest threats to the organization as it is today can spark a powerful discussion that creates energy and a shared sense of urgency.

The second step is to examine each influence in the external environment from an offensive perspective of opportunities and advantage to seize. Begin by asking which trends are most likely to present a positive strategic advantage and which trends will open a breakaway from the competition—an opportunity to extend and strengthen the organization's reach and position in the marketplace and improve its value. Delve deeper into your team's thinking and assumptions about what creates opportunity by asking each individual to silently consider this question: "What is the single greatest opportunity open to our organization?" Ask which element of the team's vision will be realized when this opportunity is seized.

What is most challenging in this scanning process is that it strictly avoids generating solutions. That is why it generates creative energy and tension. Nowhere in the discussion thus far has the question of how emerged. In fact, it is important to keep out of the discussion statements about what needs to be done and which actions to take. The focus of this conversation is to harness the group's energy in selling opportunities and selling problems, not on generating solutions.

Focusing on the Internal Drivers

A key internal driver is something that is occurring today that is likely to continue in the future if unabated. Now take a second look at the group's description of the internal organization and compare and contrast its current state to the desired future state. If no change occurs in the strategy, structure, technology, and human resource policies, how are these elements likely to play out over the course of time?

The outcome of a scan of the big picture in which you and your team will deliver results is threefold. First, you and your team have identified the external and internal factors that are most likely to push and pull your organization as a whole and your initiative in particular. By broadening and lengthening your collective perspective and then refining your focus, you have converged on the essential variables you will need to continuously observe and analyze. Second, this big picture scan answers the question, "Why change?"—the business case or rationale for change. You have identified the urgent realities that make the status quo or business as usual dangerous and fraught with potential loss. You have also identified an attractive and compelling future with distinct benefits to you, your team, the organization, and its stakeholders.

Knowing why helps mitigate the sense of feeling like part of a moving target. Knowing your organization's drivers improves your organizational savvy. Finally, and perhaps most important in regard to influence, facilitating a scan engages your team in strategic critical thinking to build a foundation of shared understanding and personal meaning.

The unique characteristics of the competitive landscape in which you want to succeed require routine scanning. Change in one element of the environment can cause a ripple effect of consequences in other related areas.

 **Appendix B**

Organizing to Influence
THE PUSH-PULL-HOW BUSINESS CASE

The elements of an influential business case are reviewed below.

- *Sell the problem (the "push"): provide urgent reasons to address this issue now.* Start with a brief overview of the problem. Connect the problem explicitly to the world and interests of the listeners. Create urgency. Provide a clear explanation of what is time sensitive about this action or initiative. Be prepared to back up your urgent claims with specific evidence, a story, facts, and credible peer comparisons. Prepare to prove the costs of delay.

- *Sell the opportunity (the "pull"): describe benefits of addressing this issue.* Clarify the organizational net benefits of or payoff to addressing this issue. State explicitly the personal benefits for your listeners. What proof do you have that your proposed approach will pay off? Back up your claims with specific evidence, facts, and examples of peers already engaged in this effort and realizing benefits.

- *Sell your approach (the "how"): provide a high-level overview of your proposed approach.* What is your plan? What is your approach to resolving the pain of the problem as outlined—starting from where you are today—and to realize the benefits? What are the specific performance goals this initiative will achieve? What are the key dependencies that involve this audience's effort and involvement? How will this initiative sustain itself over time (sources of funding, maintenance, impact on human resources, and so on). Emphasize agreements, that is, on what critical points do you already agree? Acknowledge fears, concerns, "counterstories," or objections to your approach. Counter the objections with an alternative perspective. Provide proof for your alternative point of view. What evidence do you have that your audience's greatest fears or objections will not materialize? Restate the critical elements of your plan at a very high level.

■ *Call for action: present immediate next steps.* Prepare for this portion of your influence strategy with the expectation of agreement. Anticipate yeses. Given agreement and acceptance, what will you do personally as immediate follow-up? What would you have members of the audience do in the next two to six weeks?

■ *Close memorably: summarize key points.* Keep in mind audiences remember beginnings and endings. What are the three key points you want this audience to remember?

 **Appendix C**

Influence Planning
LAST-MINUTE CHECKLIST

Here are some important questions to ask yourself before walking out the door.

- *Audience role:* Who is my audience? What role does each person on the call or in the meeting play in the decision-making or implementation process?

- *Meeting goal:* What is my goal for this particular encounter? To solicit input or information? To obtain feedback? To gain access or a personal referral to someone else? To persuade someone to have a favorable attitude toward my project? To obtain authorization for resources? To gain endorsement? To make a favorable decision? Obtain help with implementation?

- *Minimal and memorable message:* What is the minimal and memorable theme of my initiative? What is the three-minute summary of my initiative, proposal, or idea?

- *My credibility:* What is the basis of my credibility with each person? How am I prepared to have my credibility in evidence? Relationships? References? Credentials? Past accomplishments? Competencies?

- *Listeners' preferred persuasion approach:* What kind of persuasion will my listeners require? Rational (analytics and evidence)? Visionary or conceptual (the larger purpose)? Personal self-interests? Political (how the initiative will appear to a larger audience)? Relational (how the initiative fits within ongoing interactions)? Authority (whether the authority in charge is being respected)?

■ *My intercultural persuasion style:* What adjustments do I personally need to make? Use a higher or lower volume? Be less or more direct? Use a faster or slower pace? Focus more or less on task or relationship? Appeal to different audiences? Demonstrate respect for authority?

■ *My language:* What might I do to be articulate, inclusive, and comprehensible in my language? What jargon will I want to avoid? What words do I want to avoid?

■ *Cultural common ground:* How might my purpose align or conflict with each person's values, norms, or beliefs? How might I bridge these differences?

■ *Congruence of interests:* How might my interests, purpose, or idea align or conflict with each person's interests? How might I bridge these differences? Offer control? Share resources or information? Clarify decision-making jurisdiction?

■ *Desired commitments:* What commitments might I ask for? What specific *action* do I want this person to take to advance my purpose or idea? (Note: Does this action require sufficient effort to signal commitment?) Who should *witness* this action? Who am I allowed to notify about this endorsement or decision?

■ *Relationship improvement:* What can I do to leave the relationship better than I found it?

 **Appendix D**

Audience Assessment Questions

Before your next important opportunity to influence others, make a list of the information you will need to know to appeal to your audience's interests, values, and practices. In addition to understanding the cross-cultural dimensions of your audience, you will want to know the answers to the questions presented below to help you effectively tailor your influence strategy in the complex international organization.

- *Pressure and feelings:* Remember that under intense time and performance pressure, even the strongest company one-culture DNA will lose to individuals' native cultures. What kind of pressure is this audience under? What are the audience's feelings and personal concerns about current changes?

- *Objections or concerns:* Who might have concerns about the goodness of your initiative? Who may feel they have something to lose if your initiative is successful? What are their personal concerns or objections to your idea or initiative? What stories are circulating that refute your claims? These contradictions are "counterstories" you will need to address and refute with your evidence.

- *Language:* What languages do the members of your audience speak? How proficient are they in English? What jargon are they used to? What words or term are most likely to cause a negative reaction and should you plan to avoid?

- *Appearance and mannerisms:* What is the culture in which your audience members live and work? What are their rules about appearance or dress in a business or social environment? What are their values regarding hierarchy and practices about showing respect in your appearance, greetings, and gestures? Your cultural intelligence—motivation to learn, observe, and mimic cultural customs—will help you make choices about what you look like, sound like, and say.

- *Preconceptions about you:* What are the prevailing spoken or unspoken beliefs, stereotypes, or judgments people in the audience might have about you (and your personal demographics), your organization, and the function or business you represent?

- *Needs and expectations:* What do the members of this audience need and expect from the time they spend with you to feel their time had been well spent?

The questions above are presented as a reminder of the critical information you will want to know about your audience as you plot your influence strategy. Failure to thoroughly identify whose trust and cooperation you will need to deliver results risks miscalculating where to put your influence energy. The unique characteristics of the international matrix organization—dual management authority, adaptable and shifting power centers, highly complex communication patterns, and a rich blend of cultural dimensions—go beyond the traditional "know your audience" rule of thumb.

Strategic Positioning

Cummings, Thomas G., and Edgar F. Huse. "Structural Design." In *Organization Development and Change*, 228–252. St. Paul, MN: West Publishing Company, 1989.

Galbraith, Jay. "Balancing Power and Defining Roles." In *Designing Matrix Organizations That Actually Work*, 75–85. San Francisco: Jossey-Bass, 2009.

Weisbord, Marvin R., ed. "Parallel Paths to Community: Equifinality in Action." In *Discovering Common Ground*, 45–54. San Francisco: Berrett-Koehler Publishers, 1992.

Cross-Cultural Know-How

Earley, P. Christopher, and Soon Ang. *Cultural Intelligence: Individual Interactions Across Cultures*. Stanford, CA: Stanford University Press, 2003.

Earley, P. Christopher, Soon Ang, and Joo-Seng Tan. *CQ: Developing Cultural Intelligence at Work*. Stanford, CA: Stanford University Press, 2006.

Earley, P. Christopher, and Elaine Mosakowski. "Cultural Intelligence." *Harvard Business Review*, October 2004.

Harzing, Anne-Wil, and Alan J. Feely. "The Language Barrier and Its Implications for HQ-Subsidiary Relationships." *International Journal of Cross-Cultural Management* 15, no. 1 (2008): 49–60.

Hofstede, Geert H., Gert Jan Hofstede, and Michael Minkov. *Cultures and Organizations: Software of the Mind.* New York: McGraw Hill, 2010.

Morrison, Terri, and Wayne A. Conaway. *Kiss, Bow, or Shake Hands.* Avon, MA: Adams Media, 2006.

Neyer, Anne-Katrin and Anne-Wil Harzing. "The Impact of Culture on Interactions: Five Lessons Learned from the European Commission." *European Management Journal* 26, no. 5 (October 2008): 325–334.

Schein, Edgar H. *The Corporate Culture Survival Guide.* San Francisco: Wiley, 1999.

―――. *Organizational Culture and Leadership.* San Francisco: Jossey-Bass, 1985.

Personal Influence and Persuasion

Bell, Sir David. "Investing in Youth: A Compelling Case for Corporate Social Responsibility." Speech given at Johns Hopkins University International MBA Programme Leaders+Legends series, Baltimore, MD, December 9, 2010. http://www.youtube.com/watch?v=pXfSMpsSrQA.

Chhokar, Jagdeep S., Felix C. Brodbeck, and Robert J. House, eds. *Culture and Leadership Across the World: The GLOBE Book of In-Depth Studies of 25 Societies.* Mahwah, NJ: Lawrence Erlbaum Associates, 2007.

Cialdini, Robert B. *Influence: The Psychology of Persuasion.* New York: William Morrow, 2007.

―――. *Influence: Science and Practice.* Boston: Allyn and Bacon, 2009.

Cohen, Allan R., and David L. Bradford. *Influence without Authority*. Hoboken, NJ: Wiley, 1990.

Corbett, Edward P. J., ed. *The Rhetoric and the Poetics of Aristotle*. Translated by W. Rhys Roberts. New York: Modern Library, 1984.

Griffin, Teressa Moore. *Lies That Limit: Uncover the Truth of Who You Really Are*. Voorhees, NJ: SoulWorks Publishing, 2010.

Kotter, John P. *Leading Change*. Boston: Harvard Business School Press, 1996.

————. *Power and Influence: Beyond Formal Authority*. New York: Free Press, 1985.

Petty, Richard E., and John T. Cacioppo. *Attitudes and Persuasion: Classic and Contemporary Approaches*. Boulder, CO: Westview Press: 1996.

Salbi, Zainab. "Women, Wartime, and the Dream of Peace." Speech given at TED Global Conference, Oxford, UK, July 2010. http://www.ted.com/talks/zainab_salbi.html.

Shell, G. R., and M. Moussa. *The Art of Woo: Using Strategic Persuasion to Sell Your Ideas*. New York: Penguin, 2007.

Trompenaars, Fons, and Charles Hampden-Turner. *Riding the Waves of Culture*. New York: McGraw-Hill, 1998.

Weisbord, Marvin R. *Productive Workplaces: Organizing for Dignity, Meaning, and Community*. San Francisco: Jossey-Bass, 1987.

Wikipedia, s.v. "Yerkes-Dodson Law," last modified February 11, 2011, http://en.wikipedia.org/wiki/Yerkes%E2%80%93Dodson_law.

Yerkes, Robert M., and John D. Dodson. "The Relation of Strength of Stimulus to Rapidity of Habit-Formation." *Journal of Comparative Neurology and Psychology* 18 (1908): 459–482. http://psychclassics .yorku.ca/Yerkes/Law/.

Collaboration and Conflict Management

Fisher, Roger, and Scott Brown. *Getting Together: Building Relationships as We Negotiate.* New York: Penguin, 1989.

Fisher, Roger, and Alan Sharp. *Getting It Done: How to Lead When You're Not in Charge.* New York: Harper Business, 1998.

Fisher, Roger, William Ury, and Bruce Patton. *Getting to Yes: Negotiating Agreement without Giving In.* New York: Penguin Books, 1991.

Thomas, K. W., and R. H. Kilmann. *Thomas-Kilmann Conflict Mode Instrument.* Mountain View, CA: CPP, 2007.

Weisbord, Marvin R., ed. *Discovering Common Ground.* San Francisco: Berrett-Koehler Publishers, 1992.

Personal Networks and Connections

Catalyst. *Connections That Count: The Informal Networks of Women of Color in the United States.* New York: Catalyst Group Reports, 2008.

———. *Creating Women's Networks.* New York: Jossey-Bass, 1999.

Cross, Rob, Stephen P. Borgatti, and Andrew Parker. "Making Invisible Work Visible: Using Social Network Analysis to Support Strategic Collaboration." *California Management Review* 44, no. 2 (Winter 2002): 25–46.

Cross, Rob, Tim Laseter, Andrew Parker, and Guillermo Velasquez. "Using Social Network Analysis to Improve Communities of Practice." *California Management Review* 49, no. 1 (Fall 2006), 32–60.

Cross, Rob, Jeanne Liedtka, and Leigh Weiss. "A Practical Guide to Social Networks." *Harvard Business Review* 83, no. 3 (March 2005).

Eagly, Alice H., and Linda L. Carli. "Women and the Labyrinth of Leadership." *Harvard Business Review*, September 2007.

Elfring, Tom, and Willem Hulsink. "Networks in Entrepreneurship: The Case of High Technology Firms." *Small Business Economics* 21 (2003): 409–422.

Larson, Andrea, and Jennifer A. Starr. "A Network Model of Organization Formation." *Entrepreneurship: Theory and Practice* 17, no. 2 (Winter 1993): 5–15.

Sabatinni, Laura. "The Shape of Things to Come—Women in Business Preparing for the Future." Panel at HSBC Centenary of International Women's Day, New York, March 8, 2011.

Notes

Introduction
1. Jay Galbraith, "Balancing Power and Defining Roles," in *Designing Matrix Organizations That Actually Work* (San Francisco: Jossey-Bass, 2009), 75–85.
2. Thomas G. Cummings and Edgar F. Huse, "Structural Design," in *Organization Development and Change* (St. Paul, MN: West Publishing Company, 1989), 228–252.

Chapter 1
1. G. Richard Shell and Mario Moussa, "Close the Sale: Commitments and Politics," in *The Art of Woo* (New York: Penguin Group, 2007), 207–233.
2. Matt. 25:29 (New Revised Standard Version).

Chapter 2
1. P. Christopher Earley, Soon Ang, and Joo-Seng Tan, *CQ: Developing Cultural Intelligence at Work* (Stanford, CA: Stanford University Press, 2006).
2. Geert H. Hofstede, Gert Jan Hofstede, and Michael Minkov, *Cultures and Organizations: Software of the Mind* (New York: McGraw Hill, 2010).
3. P. Christopher Earley and Soon Ang, *Cultural Intelligence: Individual Interactions Across Cultures* (Stanford, CA: Stanford University Press, 2003), 63.
4. Earley, Ang, and Tan, "Directing Your Energy: The Motivational Basis of CQ," in *CQ: Developing Cultural Intelligence at Work*, 61–81.

5. Anne-Katrin Neyer and Anne-Wil Harzing, "The Impact of Culture on Interactions: Five Lessons Learned from the European Commission," *European Management Journal* 26, no. 5 (October 2008): 325–334.

6. Figure 1 incorporates and adapts select cultural dimensions found in the following sources: Hofstede, Hofstede, and Minkov, *Cultures and Organizations*; Fons Trompenaars and Charles Hampden-Turner, *Riding the Waves of Culture* (New York: McGraw-Hill, 1998); and Jagdeep S. Chhokar, Felix C. Brodbeck, and Robert J. House, eds., *Culture and Leadership Across the World: The GLOBE Book of In-Depth Studies of 25 Societies* (Mahwah, NJ: Lawrence Erlbaum Associates, 2007).

7. R. J. House, et al., "Cultural Influences on Organizational Leadership," in *Culture, Leadership, and Organizations: The GLOBE Study of 62 Societies*, ed. Robert J. House et al. (Thousand Oaks, CA: Sage Publications, 2004), 53–54; and C. Brodbeck, S. Chhokar, and R. J. House, "Culture and Leadership in 25 Societies: Integration, Conclusions, and Future Directions," in *Culture and Leadership Across the World*, ed. Chhokar, Brodbeck, and House, 1023-1084.

8. From Neyer and Harzing, "The Impact of Culture on Interactions"; and Earley, Ang, and Tan, "Succeeding in Global Work Assignments," in *CQ: Developing Cultural Intelligence at Work*, 124–149.

9. Neyer and Harzing, "The Impact of Culture on Interactions," 5.

10. Early and Ang, *Cultural Intelligence*, 64–66.

Chapter 3

1. Richard E. Petty and John T. Cacioppo, *Attitudes and Persuasion: Classic and Contemporary Approaches* (Boulder, CO: Westview Press: 1996).

2. Roger Fisher and Scott Brown, *Getting Together: Building Relationships as We Negotiate* (New York: Penguin, 1989), 36.

3. Edward P. J. Corbett, ed., "Book I: Chapter 2, Aristotle, Rhetoric," in *The Rhetoric and the Poetics of Aristotle*, trans. W. Rhys Roberts (New York: Modern Library, 1984).

4. Zainab Salbi, "Women, Wartime, and the Dream of Peace," speech given at TED 2010 Global Conference, Oxford, UK, July 2010, http://www.ted.com/talks/zainab_salbi.html.

5. Marvin R. Weisbord, ed., "Parallel Paths to Community: Equi-finality in Action," in *Discovering Common Ground* (San Francisco: Berrett-Koehler Publishers, 1992), 45–54.

6. Paula A. Kerger, "The Future of Public Broadcasting," speech given at Johns Hopkins University International MBA Programme Leaders+Legends series, Baltimore, MD, January 25, 2011.

7. Marvin R. Weisbord, "The Learning Organization: Lewin's Legacy to Management," in *Productive Workplaces: Organizing for Dignity, Meaning, and Community* (San Francisco: Jossey-Bass, 1987), 88–105.

8. Robert M. Yerkes and John D. Dodson, "The Relation of Strength of Stimulus to Rapidity of Habit-Formation," *Journal of Comparative Neurology and Psychology* 18 (1908): 459–482, http://psychclassics.yorku.ca/Yerkes/Law/. For a translation in the vernacular, go to http://en.wikipedia.org/wiki/Yerkes%E2%80%93Dodson_law.

9. Sir David Bell, "Investing in Youth: A Compelling Case for Corporate Social Responsibility," speech given at Johns Hopkins University International MBA Programme Leaders+Legends series, Baltimore, MD, December 9, 2010, http://www.youtube.com/watch?v=pXfSMpsSrQA.

Chapter 4

1. Russ Forrester and Helen Baxter-Southworth, The Peer Collaboration Valued Behavior Rating Scale (Columbia, MD: HBS & Associates, LLC, 2003). Forrester and I began developing this list of behaviors and a measurement instrument by scanning the literature on collaboration. Among the more prominent authors were James Tamm and Ronald Luyet (*Radical Collaboration*, New York: Harper Business, 2004), Vera John-Steiner (*Creative Collaboration*, Oxford: Oxford University Press, 2000), M. T. Hansen and M. Nohria ("How to Build Collaborative Advantage," *Sloan Management Review* 46, no. 1, Fall 2004: 22–30), Charles Ehin ("Fostering Both Sides of Human Nature: The Foundation of Collaborative Relationships," *Business Horizons* 41, no. 3, 1999: 15–25), and M. E. Haskins, J. Liedtka, and J. Rosenblum ("Beyond Teams: Toward an Ethic of Collaboration," *Organizational Dynamics* 26, no. 4, Spring 1998: 34–50.

We also reviewed the literature on a closely related concept, cooperation, which has been studied extensively by Morton Deutsch and Robert Axelrod.

Our conclusion based on the review is that there is no standard, universally accepted definition of the term "collaboration." Most writers start with the dictionary definition and the plain meaning "working together." There is no consensus on the specific behaviors that determine the effectiveness of collaboration. However, there is considerable overlap in the frameworks of the various authors. We selected the framework used by Tamm and Luyet with its five principal terms: collaborative intention, truthfulness, self-accountability, self-awareness and awareness of others, and problem solving and negotiation. This framework was representative of the mainstream of the literature, balancing simplicity and completeness. The terms of the Tamm-Luyet framework were a fairly faithful reflection (in reverse) of the terms used by Patrick M. Lencioni in *The Five Dysfunctions of a Team* (San Francisco: Jossey-Bass, 2002). In light of the compatibility of the two frameworks and the benefits of having mutually reinforcing definitions, we revised the scale so that the current version contains five items based on the five behaviors suggested by Lencioni to avoid the common dysfunctions and employs a five-point frequency scale ranging from "seldom" to "usually."

2. Deanne N. Den Hartog, "Assertiveness," in *Culture, Leadership, and Organizations: The GLOBE Study of 62 Societies*, ed. Robert J. House et al. (Thousand Oaks, CA: Sage Publications, 2004) 395–436; Catalyst, *Different Cultures, Similar Perceptions: Stereotyping of Western European Business Leaders* (New York: Catalyst Group Reports, 2006); and Catalyst, *Women "Take Care," Men "Take Charge:" Stereotyping of U.S. Business Leaders Exposed* (New York: Catalyst Group Reports, 2005.

3. Adapted from K. W. Thomas and R. H. Kilmann, *Thomas-Kilmann Conflict Mode Instrument* (Mountain View, CA: CPP, 2007).

4. House, et al., "Cultural Influences on Organizational Leadership"; and Brodbeck, Chhokar, and House, "Culture and Leadership in 25 Societies."

5. Galbraith, "Balancing Power and Defining Roles."

Chapter 5

1. Tom Elfring and Willem Hulsink, "Networks in Entrepreneurship: The Case of High Technology Firms," *Small Business Economics* 21 (2003): 409–422.
2. Andrea Larson and Jennifer A. Starr, "A Network Model of Organization Formation," *Entrepreneurship: Theory and Practice* 17, no. 2 (Winter 1993): 5–15.
3. Ibid.
4. Alice H. Eagly and Linda L. Carli, "Women and the Labyrinth of Leadership," *Harvard Business Review,* September 2007, Reprint R0709C p. 9.
5. Catalyst, *Creating Women's Networks* (New York: Jossey-Bass, 1999); and Catalyst, *Connections That Count: The Informal Networks of Women of Color in the United States* (New York: Catalyst Group Reports, 2008); and Laura Sabatinni, "The Shape of Things to Come—Women in Business Preparing for the Future" (panel member at HSBC Centenary of International Women's Day, New York, March 8, 2011). Dr. Sabatinni is coleader, Work-Life Issue Specialty Team, at Catalyst.
6. Rob Cross, Stephen P. Borgatti, and Andrew Parker, "Making Invisible Work Visible: Using Social Network Analysis to Support Strategic Collaboration," *California Management Review* 44, no. 2 (Winter 2002): 25–46.

Conclusion

1. Chhokar, Brodbeck, and House, eds., *Culture and Leadership Across the World,* 1021.

Appendix A

1. Michael George, "Strategies for Winning in the Digital Commerce Age," speech given at Johns Hopkins University International MBA Programme Leaders+Legends series, Baltimore, MD, November 23, 2010.

Index

About the Author

Helen Baxter-Southworth works with leaders at all levels in Fortune 500 and international companies as well as a variety of business start-ups and nonprofit organizations. She owns and manages HBS & Associates, LLC, which she established in 1989 to provide executive coaching, change leadership consultation, and executive development programs. She is a member of the original international Women's Leadership Collaboration and continues her desire to serve women as they develop their strength, purpose, and confidence. Helen is passionate about supporting those who serve children and adults infected and affected by HIV in South Africa through the Thembalitsha Foundation. Helen lives in Ellicott City, Maryland, with her family.

You can visit Helen at her website at http://hbsassoc.com. Learn more about the Thembalitsha Foundation at http://www.thembalit sha.org.za.